JACKSON & MAIN

Also by Lindy Barr Batdorf:

Stop and Smell the Asphalt:
Laughter and love along the highway of parenthood.

Coming soon:
The Dreamer's Book of Secrets
A handbook for creative souls
and
Heartsounds:
A journey of Hope and Healing

~

Contact information:

Batdorf Communications
P.O. Box 3054
Clackamas, OR 97015

Facebook:
Jackson & Main: *Meditations and Everyday Miracles*

~

Photography by Lindy Barr Batdorf

To my dear
friend,
Jacquie —

So many sweet
memories — so
many smiles...
Do you see your
beautiful heart
within these
pages? I do....

Much Love —

JACKSON & MAIN

Meditations and Everyday Miracles

Two decades, one window and a life-changing view

Lindy Barr Batdorf

Published by:

Elk Mountain Books
Battleground, Washington

Copyright © 2019 by Lindy Barr Batdorf
Print Edition, ISBN 10: 154121949X
ISBN-13: 9781541219496

For Alan, Jode and Andy

Listen to your life.
See it for the fathomless mystery it is.
In the boredom and pain of it,
no less than in the
excitement and gladness:
touch, taste, smell your way to the holy
and hidden heart of it,
because in the last analysis
all moments are key moments,
and
life itself is grace.

Frederick Buechner

Table of Contents

Jackson & Main is a real place with real people.

The stories are all true, but small changes have been made in order to respect the privacy of individuals represented within these pages.

Acknowledgements

Hugs and many heartfelt thanks to:

My wonderful Alan, husband of 37 years and handsome, fancy boyfriend for 40, this book would not exist if you had not asked, *Hey, what happened on Jackson and Main today?* You are my toughest, best critic and for you to believe in this book showed me I could believe in it, too.

Sons Joseph and Andy, for your encouragements over time, for insisting the book come out of the drawer years ago and for reminding me it's never too late to do what I might have done.

My dear mother-in-law Fernie Maria first suggested a little place on a corner to eat and offered to watch my little boys so I could get away and think; my mom, Helen, my dad, Joe and my brother Tim all encouraged me greatly. Tim gave me the idea that this could be a book. Thank you…I miss and love you all.

My sisters, Lene, Cass and Shirl, thanks hosers, and I love-a, love-a, love-a yoooo!

Patricia Rushford for first believing.

Maxine Marsolini and Tom Fuller, for your professional insights, limitless faith and patience over many years.

Editor/publisher, Perry P. Perkins for his friendship, help and assorted, random kicks in the rear.

Wm. Paul Young, whose friendship inspired me and whose brilliant, heartfelt writings freed my own.

And…

I made my first visit to the little restaurant on Jackson and Main fresh from meeting workshop leader, Heather (Harpham) Kopp at the OCW writer's conference and reading her book, *I Went to the Animal Fair*. Her friendship and honest, visceral voice influenced me deeply and encouraged me to see and record the world differently than I ever had before.

Professional writers, editors, critique group members and friends who gave eyes-on-manuscript help or offered thoughts, ideas, opinions and encouragement during the 20-year process (including, but certainly not limited to): Sue Engelfried, Bill Dolan, Terry Whalin, Chip MacGregor, Stanley Baldwin, Geneva Iijima, Lenore Buth, Cris Oliver Ortman, the late Joe Ryan, Helen and David Haidle, Margie Boulé, Denny Soetart, Charlene Raley Poston, Mona Kruger, Cheryl Rehklau, Mokihana White, Carol Charnstrom and all "the girls," Linda Moxley, Sandy Nigro, Stan Christie, Robert Walker, Jeff Ekdahl, Caroline Manning, Laurie Dahl, Christy Botkin Reeves, Sharon Konstantin, Joannie Schrader, Joy Olander, Janet Daschel, Carole Elsen, Norm Maves, many friends at OCW and elsewhere and especially all the people who passed by a special window over the course of 20-some years, I thank you.

I shared a chapter here and a chapter there with many people over almost three decades now and I no longer have access to files sent from many. Because you are all so valuable to this final product, a Facebook page for Jackson & Main was created, inviting both friends from the past and those just now discovering our magical place to meet.

If you have been or would like to be part of the continuing experience of Jackson & Main, please visit us there and drop me a line. I'd love to hear from you. Just type in the title: **Jackson & Main: Meditations and Everyday Miracles**.

To all, and to you, dear reader, I am deeply grateful.

JACKSON & MAIN

Meditations and Everyday Miracles

Preface

The Beginning

Why come back to same chair at the same window in the same restaurant on the same corner for over two decades? Something strange or incredible always happened and I returned to find those somethings again.

I was never disappointed.

I first came in with the intent to do a simple writing exercise, but fifteen minutes in, I was so astounded I couldn't speak, just leaned back, put down my pen, closed my journal and stared out the window, stunned at what had occurred both outside the window and inside of me.

There was no set pattern or regularity to my visits, but every time I sat in my same window seat overlooking the junction of Jackson & Main Streets in a town that could be anywhere, something touching, thought provoking or strange happened, so I came back.

It was as if I had been given a silent invitation at just the right time to witness these simple, profound events; some, touching my life in broad strokes, others in soft, subtle ways. My visits there became open-eyed, live prayers and meditations on the world around me. My perceptions of that world would never be the same.

One by one, year after year, the journal entries added up and are now this peculiar memoir of life through a café window you've stumbled upon.

I encourage you to read one story at a time, then sit back with a cup of something and bring your own thoughts inside the story. *There's room after each chapter for you to write a few things, doodle, press flowers or reflect on the story as you bring your own thoughts into it.* I highly encourage you to do so. Make this book your own.

Whether this book is used to refresh the mind, reflect or meditate on life; whether it is used as a tool for writers, classrooms or a means to spark conversations, it is my hope, whatever stage of life you are experiencing, you will bring your own beautiful thoughts and unique views in to the pages and join our celebration of everyday miracles

See you in the intersections,

~Lindyb

Sidewalk Magic

*I am beginning to learn that it is the sweet, simple
things of life,
which are the real ones after all.*

~ Laura Ingalls Wilder

Springtime

A woman and her daughter walk by my window.

Some tread differently when walking with a child, this woman is one of them. Her face is open and relaxed; her pace does not scream *busy* and the child's arm is not tugged. The walk is slowed to little-leg speed.

Mom is dressed in heels and stylishly tailored office attire for the busy executive, but she is wholly absorbed in her child.

All at once, Woman and Child both bend down to examine some amazing treasure inhabiting the sidewalk. A tiny finger points, they look at one another with open-mouthed amazement as the mother bends down and crouches—they both are enraptured by what must be some kind of bug.

There is no pontificating done by The Woman, no lectures on features of the exoskeleton or life in a colony. No anxious looks at wristwatch, foot tapping or heavy sighs at the imposition of stopping.

Just silence.

Looking.

Smiling.

Wide eyes, amazed at the wonder of living and a creature so delightful and small.

It's clear The Woman has purposed to see through her daughter's new eyes and this common thing has become a delight to both.
The Child looks up and grins, The Woman smiles, stands, reaches again for a little hand and walks away with a beautiful brown-eyed reminder of her childhood who is taking tiny steps right beside her.

They are quiet, connected, and their love is very loud.

How my life or thoughts intersect...

Golden Life Walking

To travel hopefully is a better thing than to arrive.

~ Robert Louis Stevenson

Late Spring

Hot and sour soup burns with a vengeance all the way down as I watch worlds pass by just outside my window.

A cool spring-watered sun touches those people I cannot. So many worlds make their way by this window. A bus stop congregation stands alone, unified in worship of solitude and cigarettes.

Cars stop at the intersection, not ten feet away. Drivers look back and forth, sigh, wave pedestrians across or charge past, perhaps with passengers of loneliness, love, fear or poverty as passengers.

So many worlds pass by.

One world at a time.

Pass by.

A sip of hot coffee and an elderly, bent woman shuffles into my immediate line of vision, right outside the window. So close, if it weren't for the glass I could touch her.

A long, hooded raincoat protects softly curled grey hair; knotted work-worn hands clutch gloves and lace handkerchief. Heavy stockings and black orthopedic shoes on swollen feet continue moving past.

So many walk right by. So many ignore her, as if she isn't there at all.

Handbag balanced on bone-thin forearm. Hat placed just so.

One step.

One step.

One step at a time will get her there. She heads in the direction of the local grocery store down the street to the left.

I imagine her day surrounds this walk, however long a walk it is, it likely feels longer than it would have years ago. She walks slowly, purposefully. I picture her getting up early in anticipation, deciding what to wear and planning her purchases.

Will she call a cab? How will she carry her things home?

Can't carry much. No, not much at all.

Slowly, she crosses the street in the direction of the grocery store and disappears around the corner. She doesn't cut across the parking lot to save steps, but walks out of sight, around the lot, the long way, all on the sidewalk.

Can't move fast enough for that parking lot.

She'll likely spend a long time, leaning on the shopping cart, list in hand.

One step. One step at a time.

She's not in a hurry.

Long before her body forced her to slow her pace I picture her doing so anyway. Wisdom born of time and living often rests in elderly eyes. Does she have company coming over this weekend? Is she in need of filling a prescription or the cupboard before the next rainstorm comes?

Seeing her makes me wonder if those who cherish her company sweeten her life or if vast loneliness taunts, causing her to wish away memories so this *right now* might not compare cruelly.

I wonder who visits her and who asks her about her life, who values the days and seasons she's seen?

Strangely, I suddenly want to be one of them, to find her and ask her to tell me stories, ask for advice about living in the eras she's seen, maybe see if she'll jot down a special recipe her mother and her mother before her passed down.

We've become so focused on beauty and youth, I daydream about standing up and shouting that *our world has it all wrong, that some are just ahead on the path, that's all…*

The media and much of our culture pays so much attention to image, youth and skin-deep attraction and a lot of us follow like sheep, ignoring age, experience and the true stuff of life.

I want her to know how much her life matters, tell her I'm sorry for the way this world tries to push aging into invisibility and that we have it all backward, that we have it all wrong, but I don't know how to shout such a thing or even whisper such a thing without frightening her.

Many minutes have passed. She must be inside the store by now but I find myself still staring at the point she walked out of view.

How often have I not looked up to see?

If we all live long and well does this mean each of us will one day walk into a veil of aging and invisibility?

Dear God, I hope not.

Right now it seems so simple.

While it has become both natural and normal to focus on clutter, busyness and noise while treasures of time live their lives and walk alone, today, right here, there's no such thing as invisibility.

All it takes—whether words are ever exchanged or not—is for just one human being to look up with the intention to truly see another.

How my life or thoughts intersect...

The Window

There is nothing insignificant in the world.
It all depends on the point of view.

~ Johann Wolfgang Von Goethe

Early Spring

This place is magic. Yet before my first visit here—in all the years I've lived here—I've never noticed this particular corner that captures so many pieces of life and places all within one.

First, there's the school. I can just make out children playing in the distance near a post-card-pretty brick schoolhouse.

They look like extras in a movie being made in a small hometown.

Kitty-corner from this little café where I sit is a bus stop in the shade of a beautiful evergreen. Other trees lift branches to the sky, scattered throughout the lawn of a two-story red brick building. It's the city hall, fire department, hometown police station and who-knows-what all rolled into one.

Directly across the street from here is a cozy-looking mom and pop furniture store and to the south, a big old bank with ornate cement benches out front in the shade of massive, muscle-man trees similar to the leafy giants that line all the streets converging on this intersection.

East of the multi-purpose City Hall is another bus stop just down the hill from the school.

It's beautiful here. I never saw that before.

Strangers mingle with friends merging with strangers bumping past family who hurry past other strangers who are walking, driving, running, riding, rolling past this Mayberry-like corner of the universe. The view from my chair at this window is of a hometown scene that could have been painted by Norman Rockwell.

It's a little difficult to describe, but somehow being in this simple, sweet piece of the world helps me realize that we're all part of a weaving in a much larger world where our lives intersect with the rest of humanity.

Just about everywhere else I go, there's something pressing to get, see or do, but not here. I come here as a kind of mini-vacation to get away from the tugging yanks of my own life. I come here to pay attention, focus outside myself, and write what I see as a writing exercise. But this feels like a lot more than just that.

Outside of those doors it's hard to slow down, sit down, observe, listen and just breathe, but sitting here feels more natural than all the rest—I want to take this moment, this memory of this peaceful world with me—don't want to leave it here or walk away and forget how full and right it is to just sit somewhere and be.

This shouldn't be the only place the should-dos fade and life becomes sweet and uncomplicated.

This corner, this window, this view—it all converges here in such a way that gently reminds me that my life is not just about me, but part of something amazing. Taking this time makes me want to live like I mean it, and like those kids up the hill in the schoolyard, to cut loose and play again.

How my life or thoughts intersect...

<u>Intersections</u>

When one life
        connects
        intersects
with another,
                Relationship
                Occurs.
That's where lives entwine and paths cross, strengthen, fuse
            touching, but different
                like
            links   on   a   chain.

What we do

      With these connections, intersections and chain links
will

          determine the
             breadth,
             strength,
             substance
             and depth

          of our existence.

It's there,
in the
crisscross patterns

and

      intersections connecting lives
         where we all

           truly

            live.

How my life or thoughts intersect...

The Man Who Sees

It is only with the heart that one can see rightly.
What is essential is invisible to the eye.

~ Antoine de Saint-Exupery

Summer

A middle-aged man with seeing-eye dog maneuvers past fireplug, curbs and bus stop. After his dog pulls back and warns of cars, the two enter the crosswalk on the north side of the intersection, pause and walk to the far side of the street using the crosswalk to the east.

It takes them a long time to get directly across the street from me. The man lets go of the dog and gestures for him to stay.

How odd. Why did he do that?

The dog obediently waits by the curb as the man slowly raises one arm, waving it out to the side as if he is feeling for something suspended in the air. He steps cautiously in the same direction, continuing to wave into the air.

What is he looking for?

He slowly continues this odd dance until he touches a tree, feels it with both hands and steps around. Now, he's waving and stepping sideways again and moves farther, farther to the right.

I wonder if he's lost, but look at the dog and remember he told the animal to stay. Just as I'm sure he's completely confused, his foot gently comes in contact with a large cement garbage can and he stops. Standing beside the garbage can, he reaches into his backpack and gathers up a wrinkled, brown paper sack that looks like a lunch bag and takes out few pop cans and some other things and throws each item into the garbage can.

He does not continue on down the same street. He does not turn and head to the bus stop or go into the furniture store.

He turns around the same way he came and goes back.

~

Some time has passed now, my coffee cup is empty and needs refilled, yet I haven't been able to get what he did out of my mind.

I've been sitting here puzzling over it.

At the time, it wasn't stirring or particularly interesting--but the more I think about it, the more amazing it becomes, like I've just watched a story unfold like petals on a rose. I haven't moved from this spot for quite some time.

It's clear he had no other business on the far side of the crosswalk other than to locate the one lone garbage can along the street and has just retraced his steps; taking the very same path back as he had taken to arrive.

Exactly the same path.

I had just witnessed this man, who could not even see the garbage he threw into the trash can, walk several blocks completely out of his way, whether anyone saw him or not, to simply do what was right.

Not long after he is out of sight, an elderly man with a sweater not unlike the one Mr. Rogers always wears, a man who looks like he's bounced a few grandkids on his knee, walks slowly up to the same trash can and after looking from one side to side to the other to see if anyone is watching, reaches inside and removes some of the things the other man had just thrown away.

He quickly sorts out what he wants and tucks it all in a cloth bag under his arm and walks down past the furniture store.

The deposit on the pop cans he retrieved from garbage can will bring him a couple of dimes for his trouble.

Dimes add up.

Little things, little right things add up.

How my life or thoughts intersect...

Stilettos and Permanent Waves

If we are to love our neighbors, before doing anything else we must see our neighbors. With our imagination as well as our eyes, ...like artists, we must see not just their faces but the life behind and within their faces.

~ Frederick Buechner

Autumn

These people are beginning to all look familiar.

There's middle-aged Mrs. Clip-Along with the young heart that defies the age her body reveals. Even from here I can see she's smiling and young on the inside. People like her may age but will never grow old.

There's Twenty-two with the baby girl who smiles and plays in the warm grass. I wonder if the weariness of motherhood weighs down on her, if she ever takes time for granted and can't feel the days just thundering past. Will Twenty-two remember this day in the life of her child and the time they spent just living and laughing, there in the warm early autumn sun or will she remember it as the day the gas payment was due or the car needed fixed? Will she succumb to the noise and pressures of life that steal vision and peace?

Is that what happens to create the ones who do grow old, holding lists of regrets inside bitter, closed hearts? Maybe they're not really closed at all.

The way the young mother smiles when her daughter laughs and watches intently when the little one tosses clover into the air makes me think they just might be destined to become two of the never-grow-old ones.

The man with the seeing-eye dog all but jogs past my vantage point today. It's been quite a while since I've been here or seen them, and it's clear they both know this street well now.

He and his dog are completely in sync—seems they know each other better now, too.

Looking to the left there is an obvious connection about to occur between two women who could not look more different, yet even as they stand on opposite sides of the crosswalk it's clear the two women are friends.

One is a slim black woman whose hair is short and tidy. She wears no make-up and her apparel is plain, understated, professional and down-to-earth.

The other woman is large, white and everything about her seems to be overstated with bright yellow hair, dark black roots, and so much make-up her appearance is clownish.

Her eyes are covered in sharp hues of shimmering blue-green eye shadow, sharp thick brows penciled in with much vigor and her cheeks are the color of pomegranate juice. All of this oddly complements leopard-print, skin-tight jeans and spiked red stilettos pinching her toes into two aching, pointing pieces of human flesh. She teeny-teeny-step/runs forward with arms flailing, in stark contrast to the other woman who takes quick, gracious steps.

They are definitely different individuals, but their expressions are the same as they clasp hands and smile broadly. They talk excitedly for a few minutes, consult wristwatches and when the time comes for them to part, they hug.

It's not just an obligatory hug, but a *God, I love this friend*, kind of hug. It refreshes me to see two people who are so different, simply love and appreciate each other.

Just as the friends part, a flower print dress and fresh permanent wave passes by them. Did Flower Print Dress get her new perm in an attempt to fit in with the others in the office?

Maybe she got it to simplify the morning routine or endured the long, smelly process of having her hair chemically curled just to make a change in a life that feels a little boring or just too predictable.

Does she have a big-smile-and-hug-on-the-street friend, too?

Print dresses, permanent waves, earth tones and leopard prints conceal bits of truth inside of them.

On Jackson and Main on a lovely bright autumn day I consider priceless things like friendship and change, and that no matter what we look like or how we may change over the years, a good friend is one of the most beautiful things we can be.

How my life or thoughts intersect...

Races, Ducks and Bubbles

*Do not forget that the value and interest of life
is not so much to do conspicuous things...
as to do ordinary things with the perception
of their enormous value.*

~ Pierre Teilhard De Chardin

Winter

No sooner have I sat down and Mr. Serious U.P.S. marches right beside Mr. Hurried Federal Express in what appears to be the start of some sort of delivery race.

Mr. Serious shoots a sideways glance to Mr. Hurried, who looks the other way and begins to walk just a little bit faster as Mr. Serious fires another quick glance at his rival and they both pick up a little speed. Testosterone and determination must have kicked in, but just as the walking race hits the crosswalk they act antsy about having to stop, listen and look both ways.

It looks like they're comparing clipboards as they walk—I wonder if they are and if they compare uniforms too and if this is a race, where's the finish line?

Over by the bus stop, Mr. Teen Coolness wearing his slanted guitar like an extra arm, walks in a slouching dance-step past

Mr. Forty-Plus who has on a new-looking backpack and jacket. Mr. Forty-Plus is portly and plain, but he looks like someone loves him.

Three unconnected people perch like birds set to roost inside the bus stop. They look sad and mournful and all are extremely careful not to talk to the other. Over time, each has learned just when to look up and when to look down in order to continue to not connect with another life form.

They are all gifted in the *Avoiding You* ballet. The steps are complicated rhythms that don't give too much away.

A group of three children arrive with mom in the lead.

Little ones don't know this dance yet, so they look right at the people in the bus stop. The youngest one even points at Mr. Coolness with the guitar and appears to make a comment that her mother quickly shushes. Mom then gives the guitar-wearer a shrug and Guitar-man tries to act as if he didn't hear the child or see the pointing finger or her mother at all.

If he thinks ignoring them might make him look even cooler, I kinda think it doesn't.

I wonder if the little girl with her innocent, out-loud observations soon learns the skill of acting like others don't matter, too.

The mother negotiates her little ducklings safely across the street. Scorn paints itself upon her brow mingled with exhaustion. Her mouth forms into an *Oops!* She turns and marches her children back to the bus stop for the retrieval of what could it be? Ah…. forgotten bus schedule.

She sighs and smiles.

A piece of her puzzle is put back into place and the visible relief remains on her face a few moments after as she instructs her little group to move onward again.

As she walks away, a bus pulls up and a rough quilting of humanity pushes itself inside the thirty-five foot articulated advertisement. A squeak, a whine of metal, a gushing sound and another bus pulls up, depositing more people who also seem to ignore one another as if this experience is not something they all share.

Who among them rides home with a good day in the hip pocket and who might be overwhelmed with a day just spent crunching numbers and dealing with attitudes and angst?

Who has a lot of neat pals at work and who just endured over eight or ten hours interfacing with challenging kinds of people who may not even know that sharing the same airspace with them is taxing.

I wonder.

How many on that bus actually had the energy or interest to connect with someone else?

How many have none left to give?

Just because someone doesn't want to chum it up in public doesn't mean they're unfriendly. We are all just different.

Not bad. Not wrong. Just different.

But wouldn't it be cool if, even in the depths of all our differences, we could keep our tender, honest children's hearts intact like these little ones or those kids in the playground up the hill?

Tapping into that kid inside might help us discover the game in things like leading a group of children down a busy sidewalk, delivering packages or even sitting on a bus after a long day suddenly become invigorating again because it feels like coming outside to play. Protective bubbles of silence might float away when we rediscover how we used to be energized just being with each other with our guards down.

Though we can't turn back the clock, even as grownups we can stop and remember that it's always been the simple things that make being part of the human race feel less like a race and so much more human.

How my life or thoughts intersect...

Little Gifts

Great things are done by a series of small things brought together.

~ Vincent Van Gogh

Autumn

It's cold today on Jackson and Main.

The shuddering few who have gone by have been bundled up, trying their best to keep warm. Not many pleasure walker-drivers today. Just those people who need to be in a place or go get a thing or two.

Here-to-there excursions only today, except one.

Just one lone, white-haired gonna-be passenger inhabits the bus stop.

It looks as if she wears several layers of clothing, the last being a bright red cardigan sweater. She holds a big canvas bag so full it bulges and overflows with things like yarn, knitting needles, assorted papers and unknown what-nots.

Red Cardigan shuffles her feet and rubs her own arms to try and keep warm.

She bends slightly and squints to read the side of the bus shelter, which appears to house a copy of the schedule.

Whatever she's looking for is difficult for her to see, because she bends closer and squints some more. She turns and sits on the bench to search through her trusty canvas bag with a *Where on earth did I leave those glasses* kind of look on her face.

She looks up from her archaeological excavation inside the tote to check her watch. Shaking her head, she sighs and begins hunting through the inner recesses of her magical bag once more, then squinting and taking a couple intermittent sidelong glances at the wall post as she does so.

Sitting there with a sweet, puzzled look on her face, she looks like someone's kind and playful aunt or cookie-baking grandma.

I imagine that handbag of hers being a kind of wonder-bag filled with all kinds of peculiar and exciting things that would keep a child busy and out of trouble for hours.

But perhaps there are no young people in her life and the child she teaches and entertains lives in her own heart.

She looks at her watch again and then in the direction from which the bus will hopefully arrive. Either it's late; she wants to keep moving to ward off the autumn chill or both, because she starts pacing and shivering once more.

A bus approaches and Red Cardigan looks up brightly. Her countenance changes as she looks quickly down. Not her bus. It glides past without stopping.

Inside the bus though, a college-age man wears headphones and it looks like he's not aware he's on a means of public transport. Even from here it's easy to see he has gone to a place of sound and wild rhythms that bounce his head and contort his expression with the pounding beat.

The world he's experiencing must be merging with the bumping and rolling felt on the bus. Either way, he makes the bus ride look fun.

Red Cardigan places her bag of mystery back on the bench and continues to pace and rub her arms through the thick layers of clothing.

She looks up suddenly and smiles at the bus rounding the corner. It lurches to a massive grinding stop as she gathers her simple things, arranges her white hair and steps onto the bus. After standing in the cold so long the warmth inside must feel wonderfully cozy as it flows over her chilled red face.

As the doors of the bus shut and the patient lady with the magical canvas bag finds comfort as well as her seat, a loud voice behind me is so startling I almost spill my coffee.

A woman is chatting at her friend and has the shrill, animated sound of someone barking at a carnival.

The woman with her volume set on high discusses in detail, her investment of both time and money in each of her ten two-inch fingernails. Loud Talker explains how her colossal claws were clipped and filed, just how much of each is fake or truly her own, how the fakes were attached, what brand of colors were used and the depth of significance all of this has to her and her psyche.

After being drawn into their conversation whether I like it or not, pieces of this day begin to glide and meld together creating a brand new treasure all its own.

As the woman drones on, her friend makes little noises like she's truly interested in the recitation of The Saga of the Fingernails with an occasional *Oh!* and *Really?*

It occurs to me it's not the thing she's talking about that's so interesting; it's the fact that it's *her friend sharing it* that makes it important to her.

I'm feeling awfully poetic about this, but it all keeps coming back to the little things. Everything that's occurred here today repeats that theme. I think of the people encountered today and consider that some of our days are bound to be cold and lonely; but these are the days uncomplicated, priceless little gifts come to the surface and matter the most.

The simple warmth of safe a ride home; music so alive it fills the heart and physically moves us; a conversation with a friend who is so close that little things like long, painted fingernails are interesting.

Tiny, stepping-stone moments like these get us by, get us through and help us see it doesn't take much light at all to warm up a cold day.

How my life or thoughts intersect...

Waste and Want

It is good to have an end to journey towards;
but it is the journey that matters in the end.

~ Ursula K. LeGuin

Winter

A wild-eyed man with a small, limp baby in a stroller rushes past the window.

Eye contact is made.

I see him. He sees me seeing him.

He is hurried. He is unhappy. He is young, deliberate and appears to be an injured soul harnessed with a tremendous weight upon his heart.

He goes quickly past my window to the Garbage Can.

The Man and the Seeing Eye Dog's Garbage can.

The Grandpa's garbage can.

The young father parks his child in the rickety-looking stroller off to the right and searches through the refuse in the trash.

No cans today.

The garbage can sits like a shrine in remembrance of the hungry, the frightened, the ignorant and the unemployed.

It seems to say, *your refuse is another's need—be careful what you throw away.*

It's getting dark, but the child has no socks, no shoes and just seeing him makes me cold and leaves me wondering how on earth I could help. I open my wallet and see I only have a few coins.

The man and his child jettison off in the direction of the school and quickly disappear as they rush off, probably in search of more garbage cans.

I wanted to do something…where did he go?

Waiting and watching, the man and his child do not come back this way.

If he'd just come back, I say to myself, *if he'd just come back, I'd go up to him, maybe, I could say or do something...*

Even as I think this again I have no idea exactly what my help would look like to the man. Again I ask myself, how could I offer help when help is not sought?

Staring out the window, darkness continues to enfold the street like a thick fog.

I watch, wait. The man and his pale child are long gone.

Just thinking about the two causes a chill to crawl up my spine. Walking to the counter to order some hot coffee I hold the money in my hand and stop when I consider the money I'm about to spend on a hot drink.

Looking back at the window, images return of the fast-moving young man with hollow eyes and his barefoot, coatless child in the shabby-looking stroller and as evening turns to night, I make my purchase.

Holding the hot cup of coffee in both hands to warm them I look again out into the darkness and consider pop cans, waste and little things that could make a world of difference.

How my life or thoughts intersect...

Dollar Bills and Dreams

Much of the social history of the Western world
over the past three decades
has involved replacing what worked
with what sounded good.

~ Thomas Sowell

Spring

The furniture store across the street has been having a moving sale almost as long as I've been coming here and now they're gone.

Business might have been bad here on this piece of the planet. Perhaps there haven't been enough numbers of people moving in and out of their doors with receipts in their pockets to support the business of selling armchairs, sofas and ottomans.

For whatever reason, a cartoon figure of an extremely happy moving man painted on the window belies any sadness that could have accompanied this move. He looks out over the street with a broad, friendly smile.

But what of the owners and what are they thinking or feeling today?

What caused this business to fold up and move on, change locations or close down? If they've expanded and bought a larger store somewhere I see no notice telling customers where to find them.

Maybe this small hometown business refused to remain current or stay on the cutting edge of all it takes today to bring in customers. Maybe people slowly stopped coming in because being a regular customer of this old friend who lives just down the street became a lot more expensive than going to the impersonal, big store who often has lots of cheaper stuff, lots of sales and less and less customer service

Did the people who owned the old furniture store think that things would always stay the same; that they would never have to change or adapt to new ideas to keep their little store full of customers? Is that why they're gone today?

I hope it's a sign of a wish fulfilled and not the result of a stubborn refusal to change or grow that caused business to dry up. I hope it's not because once-regular customers and neighborhood friends stopped coming by because they were willing to trade quality to save a couple bucks.

If that's the case, it just doesn't sound like good business to exchange things that are priceless for things that are not.

Could this be a dream in the dust or a wonderful new beginning?

Maybe it's both.

How my life or thoughts intersect...

Invisible View

*Better keep yourself clean and bright:
you are the window through which you must see
the world.*

~ George Bernard Shaw

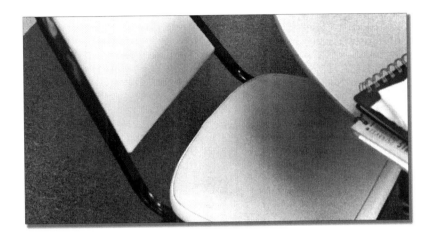

Autumn

A hurried, anxious man is busy cleaning the restaurant windows right in front of me. It looks like he's washing the windows as if his life and breath depend on it.

Maybe it does.

As he carefully replaces a suction cup supported sign and squeegees off the glass, he slaps a big glass of soda on the table right in front of me, possibly as a way of saying, *You are invisible*, or maybe *I have no observable social skills*.

Perhaps it entails a little of each.

When he's finished, I make a mental note that the windows look nice but he looks kind of fussy, a little angry and maybe a little insane.

He has scrubbed up my view here on Jackson and Main and that's mighty nice of him. I offer him a hearty *thank-you* and tell him that he did a fine job. He is visibly pleased that I noticed his work, but doesn't say anything, just clamps his lips together and gives a ¼ nod in my general direction.

I didn't tell him that I also noticed that the only time he dropped anything, or acted less than confident, was the split second his boss peered out of the back room, looking strange and suspicious, to check up on him.

And I also didn't offer up the opinion on the whole sanity thing because I really didn't think he was out of his mind, and even if I did, that wouldn't be something to just bark out at a person.

Actually, it seems more likely that, for whatever reason, he's just a little out of sync with the rest of the world—like everyone else on the face of the earth at one time or another.

Dreamer or not, lost or not, sane or not—what's clear is that whatever made him angry in the first place still lives inside his eyes.

How my life or thoughts intersect...

The Joust

*Two roads diverged in a wood, and I—I took
the one less traveled by,
and that has made all the difference.*

~ Robert Frost

Summer

A teenager drives past in a hot looking car with the essence of cool practically painted on the doors. He sports a pair of *Look at me but don't laugh,* sunglasses and he obviously enjoys the feel of his hat on backwards.

A kind of joust occurs in the intersection right outside today.

The youth and his cherry red sports car steadily approach the intersection in front of the has-been furniture store, at the exact same time an older gentleman with his hat on forward with a pair of *I can see better with these on,* glasses approaches from the opposite direction.

There is a moment of uncertainty as to who got there first and who might have the right-of-way. Something inside causes me to assume the teenager is going to blast right past the old gentleman, as cocky kids are wont to do.

This boy surprises me.

Even with an attitude that would have him drape his arm out the window *just so*, he stops and waits for the older man to go first.

The gentleman waves a heartfelt thank-you and smiles at the boy.

The fingers on the young man's lazy-looking hand move slowly and ever so slightly, just enough that he acknowledges the thank-you, but not enough to blow his image.

Even so, I see a piece of his heart.

How my life or thoughts intersect...

The Dream Man

Whatever you do, or dream you can,
begin it.
Boldness has genius and power and
magic in it.

~ Johann Wolfgang von Goethe

Summer

Something happened that I simply don't understand.

It's an extremely hot summer day today, and I passed an extremely thin, frail man pushing and pulling a massive, heavy load, several miles from here as I drove to my special corner.

Surprisingly, at this very moment, that same man is making his way past this window, still battling the huge pile of boxes tied and strapped to a creaky little cart. He pauses long enough to peel off his sleeveless t-shirt, wipe his face and take a long breath before he continues onward.

As he comes closer, I see he is not only terribly thin, but he is also quite old. This slight, elderly man has just walked at least three miles to get to this corner, and what he pushes and pulls on the mover's cart is as tall as he is and looks ten times as heavy.

This scene is almost too symbolic of the struggles and stresses inflicted upon us by life.

Where on earth is he going with such a thing?

What's in there that's worth such punishment to move?

I simply have to know.

Quickly grabbing up my things, I take a last slurp of soda and rush out the door, gasping as I breathe in the hot summer air.

I cross the street to catch up, wishing I'd worn something lighter, or at least a pair of walking shoes.

I'm off to investigate…

The man negotiates his huge load all the way up a steep hill past the school. I stealthily follow him, pretending to be a busy pedestrian urgently on my way to somewhere incredibly important. By now, I'm even more determined to know where he's going, what's inside those heavy boxes and why he is going wherever he is going in the first place.

Thinking he couldn't be venturing too much further, I neglect to bring my car. He ventures a *great deal further*, and here I am, wearing bad shoes, looking more and more like a nuthatch and less and less like an important person with pressing and essential things to do.

After limping along at a nice clip I am able to close the gap between us at an intersection at what feels like a mile or more past Jackson and Main. I wipe the dust from my eyes, hoping I don't look too stalker-like and nervously approach him at the crosswalk as he waits for the light to change.

Working up my nerve, I clear my throat and offer a hearty hello along with some inane chatter about the doggone heat.

His weary face brightens to a broad smile and he returns my hello. He tells me his name is George. I clumsily ask how he can stand to push such a heavy load so far on such a sweltering day.

He pats the boxes and says the cargo is comprised of precious supplies he was given for his boat. *It's a boat I've been fixin' up*, he says, adding he has absolutely no way to get her into the water.

No trailer, no more money, and that's all that, he says as he sighs and before I can absorb what he's just said, he takes a fresh bag of corn chips out of his pack and hands them my way, thanking me for asking. I thank him right back, open the chips and grab a handful.

There we stood in the hot sun beside a huge bunch of boat supplies tied to a small pull-cart resting beside the road, crunching corn chips and discussing the impossible.

In that moment, I fell in love with the whole world.

This man has a dream.

This man is not giving up on that dream.

This man does not give up on his dream even though the odds are against it ever coming true.

I try to imagine what it is that keeps him going and realize the force compelling him to walk and push and shove at the huge load for such a long distance, despite his age, is hope.

Perhaps he can feel the fluid freedom of floating along, unencumbered there on the cool, clear water, as he struggles now with all it takes to see his vision become reality.

Maybe he knows the more obstacles removed from his impossible dream, the more possible it becomes.

Before turning to come back, I ask for his phone number in case I am able to locate someone who could help him get his boat on the river. He smiles again, locates a scrap of paper in his pocket. He scrawls down his information and shakily hands it to me. I put the number in my pocket, thank him for the chips and fine conversation and tell him good luck and goodbye.

I didn't notice the paper flutter out of my pocket and float away; didn't know it was gone until I arrived back at my car and began my search through pockets, purse, car and sidewalk for it.

Now, back in the cool air-conditioned space of the small café, I look up toward the hill where George shared his corn chips and the reason for his journey. It's then that I realize I don't even know where he was heading with that load, or how much farther he had to go.

Maybe I'll see the thin old man with the youthful dream again—and if I do, I hope to God he's on that river.

How my life or thoughts intersect...

Envelopes and Arteries

The price of anything
is the amount of life you exchange for it.

~ Henry David Thoreau

Late Summer

A businessman has removed his tie, signaling the end of a long, hard day. He holds a leather envelope tightly to his side, I wonder if it brims with worries to carry home, possible fuel for a heart attack; the kind of sneaking thing that creeps up slowly, leather envelope by leather envelope until sometime, somewhere and someplace down the road, the body implodes against itself, simply saying, *enough*.

The furniture store is still empty.

Doesn't appear to have been sold yet, though it's been an awfully long time.

Cars pass by.

Like activity in arteries.

No signs left of the community carnival that was here just last week. The streets were closed for rides, games and booths as potential customers were called over to destroy balloons, squirt wooden clowns in the mouth or throw baseballs at milk bottle-shaped chunks of cement to win plastic toys and little stuffed animals. Others tried to entice the wandering crowd over to their booth to buy crafts, plants or the latest miracle of multi-level marketing.

There were ponies here, too.

Hot ponies.

Ponies that walked 'round and 'round with one squirming, carnival-worn child after another hoisted on top of the creatures' sweating backs. I felt sorry for the exhausted animals as well as the "operator" of the ride because he had the same look in his eye as the ponies.

The sweet cinnamon memory-smell of hand-made elephant ears is gone and it its place, the rich scent of hot coffee and homemade soup that sit on the table before me today.

I remember little girls over on a makeshift stage in the grass under the big pine tree by City Hall. The girls in sequins and leotards, tap-tap-tapping and grinning their energy away on a hot summer day dancing to the recorded sounds of show tunes and some melodies I couldn't quite place.

Watching the crowd I notice the older the child, the less *oohs, ahs,* and *aw-ws*.

Tiny little tap dancers flub and cringe, misstep and get off beat, yet the audience like one big person with one big agreeable personality, grins.

But the moment the older girls, the girls with more ability and grace start clicking heels with deft precision, the crowd notably turns; even shifts and loses attention, focusing instead on things in the grass, what they are eating or anything else that might be handy. It looked like only moms, dads and grandparents are still entranced, elbowing each other, pointing and nodding vigorously.

After watching a while I realize it's not the performance they see when the little ones take the stage, it's not the accuracy or abilities of the performer placed in high regard; it's innocence.

106

Innocence.

It's the pure smile and the untouched heart, it's the absence of vanity, pride, ego, ambition or selfish motive that wins hearts and garners the biggest applause.

Stopping to think about it, it seems that's true for the rest of life, too. The traffic at the intersection continues to stop and go, stop and go, stop and go.

Other children and students on summer leave from the rigors of school go past my window on scooters and bikes while the buses stop in a metallic symphony of sound, empty themselves and lock and reload.

When I picture the town carnival and its echoes of music and children dancing in the warm summer sun, all the rush-rush in the world slows as images of last week's street fair peek in through my favorite window, where still life thrives and becomes animated, and for this one sweet, beautiful moment, this living tapestry is awash in the bright warmth of summer and alive with hope and innocence.

Innocence.

That's the pure, bright place perhaps we all hope to find again.

How my life or thoughts intersect...

Human Billboards

Life loves to be taken by the lapel and told:
'I am with you kid. Let's go.'
~Maya Angelou

Summer

Hard to believe it's been almost two years since my last visit here. Today is a blazing, hot summer day with temperatures breaching the hundred-degree mark.

Skate-boarders attempt to cool themselves in the hot wind as they cruise past the window, most with their attitudes perched firmly atop their boards. One such attitude sports a bright new t-shirt with the words *Shut up, BITCH!!* written in large block letters on the back.

My heart aches for this boy.

What happened along the road he rides that would make him a human billboard for such a sentiment?

Not only is he willing to wear it, but he probably saw it in a store, realized it would affect someone close to him, pulled out his precious teenager's wallet and parted with some even more precious teenager's money in order to buy it, wear it and tell us all something deep.

Is he just being rebellious or is it more than that?

A hurt perhaps?

A wound?

Maybe he thought of someone like me, sitting in a restaurant on Jackson and Main and just wanted to shock me.

Young man—it doesn't shock me. It makes me wonder when was the last time someone listened to you, really looked into your eyes and listened.

I wonder if it's all just teenage angst or if anyone has ever cared enough to look inside and find out who really lives inside this strange and changing you.

As the young man disappears out of view, the unexpected combination of pity and grief he brought in remains.

Are people more likely to display anger and bitterness people who are just wounded, afraid and want to be loved? Or do they just want to be noticed?

I wonder...

It's not long before another skateboarder, who is busy negotiating the sidewalk surf, glides by. He wears a bright blue backpack and a baseball cap worn to keep the sun out of his eyes.

He is much younger.

His shirt has no message, just a t-shirt with a few stains on the front from being a kid, a kid who likes to play outside and eat sticky, colorful sweet things.

He's a boy having fun, just rolling along looking for life's next big wonderful summer adventure.

Looks like hormones, life and attitude haven't hit him or hurt him   yet.

How my life or thoughts intersect...

Little Big Somethings

Everything flows; nothing remains.

~ Heraclitus

Late Summer

A truck passes by, loaded to overflowing with, what—the contents of someone's house? No, looks like camping gear and recreational equipment. Two or three coolers, and one of those four-wheel vehicles, poised ready to pounce into the wild.

What good or bad memories will be made with the use of these things?

A bus pulling away from the bus stop heaves and moans under the personage pressure. Hot people in hot cars are all busy experimenting with the greenhouse effect.

Soggy, scowl-wearing, frustrated people are in the cars with the windows open. Cool, collected primroses calmly blossom inside the autos with the windows rolled up.

Funny, it would seem to be the other way around.

And isn't that just a little like us...

But with us it's emotions we're keeping inside. The bigger the feeling, the more pressure there is to roll the windows up.

Some of us learn over time how to fit in and not give much away.

Little clues show, but the rest is supposed to get tucked inside.

The thing is, we give off those little clues in absolutely everything we do.

We offer them in the things we wear or carry with us, and even what we choose to move about in can share sweet little somethings about who is inside—or at least an image of who we'd like to be.

There goes a practical mom-mobile, a van with child car seats and sticky handprints on windows; here's a new graduate with tassel proudly displayed on the rear-view mirror of a car that wasn't cool when his grandparents owned it but it sure is now, because it's his.

A man with bad case of midlife crisis stops at the intersection in a lot of money; a bicycle built for one rolls awkwardly down the sidewalk with two flailing, laughing junior high kids astride and a motorcycle thunders to a stop, shouting bits of no-nonsense, information in chrome and black leather as it revs up and rumbles past the window.

And let's not forget the ever-popular bumper sticker.

These are proof that some person took time out of his or her life to shop, purchase and apply an adhesive message just to share their inner reflections.

Like the person who stuck it there wanted to say, *I just want to paste something from my inside to the outside of this vehicle without any comment from you.* It's a pretty safe way to yell or laugh with the world passing by.

Someone's child is an honor student somewhere.

Several want to let us know that they had the money, time and energy to go to a tourist attraction.

A station wagon pulls up and someone taped a big wide sign on the back window to tell us about a famous evangelist who's heading this way.

One person wants to advertise the fact that they supported the loser in the last presidential election. Maybe they're not lazy, just trying to send a message to those who voted for the winner, like *I bet you're kinda sorry now* ...

Just as cars and trucks are covered in messages, so are the faces of those who walk by my looking-glass window.

People who are alone are generally frozen-faced.

People with friends are usually animated and laughing, though there are those who look like they're in the middle of a fight or completely bored in the company of the other.

Normally, no one looks inside here, but even when they do, they always act like I'm invisible. But today, two, now make that three people actually looked inside and smiled directly at me!

When did it become unusual to smile at other people?

I grew up in a small town, and it wasn't unusual then or there. I don't usually come in this time of day so maybe it's just an absence of glare on the glass, but something is definitely different because no one has ever done that before.

I don't know why they're doing it, but I like it.

Of all the little bits and pieces shared by those who go by this window, this simple, pleasant, silent communication from one human being to another is one that could actually change the world a little if we all decided to practice it regularly.

Yes, our transportation and attire advertise thoughts or things we value, but what I saw in the faces of those who walked by today is more powerful than any ego echoes or bumper stickers. One is just one-way communication and the other is a real human connection.

I'd be hard-pressed to describe the clothes, age, hair color, skin color, brand of shoes or anything else about those who walked by today, but I can still see and feel the warmth of their smiles.

I'm pretty sure I'll remember those.

How my life or thoughts intersect...

Change and Crazy Music

If music be the food of love,
play on.

~ William Shakespeare

Autumn

Thunderclouds gather overhead today. Summer warmth lingers, waiting to be driven away by autumn's wild gusts of swirling, passionate color. It's a strange, but beautiful day.

The fire truck has its lights on, no siren, just backing into the station, but gee, the firemen look awfully proud of her.

The furniture store, after all this time, is still in a state of empty. No signs of life in there today except for a group of women who meet under the covered display windows outside.

They laugh, wave arms, smile and discuss something that must be pretty funny because they all take turns giggling, one holds her sides as laughter escapes her like crazy music, the high notes, I can hear even inside here.

Just now from different corners, a diverse array of men and women all meet at one time at the bus stop, some seemingly entranced by the noise and sweet sounds emanating from large headphones attached to various-shaped music machines.

Past the far bus stop, up on the hill, I can see the school is gearing up after the echoing emptiness of summer. I imagine classrooms brimming with nervous children and pre-adults, all doing their best to hide any fear or tender awkwardness.

As if on cue, three teenage boys walk by the window with books in hand and turn the corner toward the library.

Close behind, three teenage girls all wearing variations of the current fad, shadow the boys and expel laughter and high-pitched giggles with every schoolgirl heartbeat.

Slices of time, priceless bits and snippets paint themselves across this window and sometimes, the sweet scenes sweep me away. Watching the students cross the street past the bus stop, I think of how quickly children grow into these pre-adult beings and how the rusty thud of change rattles our lives.

Strange how thoughts drift, but as my eyes follow the students walking toward school I wonder if they felt as I did, that childhood and summer would last forever; and here they are again, older and facing a new school year. It's our nature to feel as if today will last forever, even though all the proof we have gathered all of our lives proves just the opposite.

When will the *forever* kind of change happen that will bring visits here to an end? Change happens to everything and everyone. To fight against change is like beating fists at the wind.

Change will come at some point or another. I'm just grateful that day is not today and that it lives forever right here.

The teenagers have disappeared around the corner and are undoubtedly nearing the library by now, and I know that before anyone knows it, one season will drift into another and a new a group of students—similar but different—will take their place.

Change.

That's just the way life moves.

Change is mingled in with the moments and it's waiting to cut in on the dance wherever we are and whatever we're doing.

Listening and watching here taught me that and so much more. It's not just being aware of the fact that change is on the way, it's being aware of the spectacular nature of this time, this now.

It's slowing down and by-God *living* the sweet simple moments that give any day a unique and special song. The jarring earthquake of change leaps in at anytime and may decide to sweep everything we have away in an instant.

Worrying about it just sours the moment and sullies the view when the time comes to look back. Seeing and knowing of life's fragility while at the same time living the moments and loving the people you share them with are what I believe what gives life sparkle.

So I'll try not to think about what might be rolling this way, whether here or my outside world. Right now, my window to the world is here, my journal is listening and my pen is in hand. The music of this moment sings a song of gratitude and God-breathed joy that rushes in like a white-water river, engulfs all the fear and what-if's, pushing them down from the surface, sweeping them far, far away.

Besides, living the little moments is what matters—this corner has helped teach me that.

All the small bits of time we've spent get deposited into The Big Bank Vault of Days and once they're added up we realize it's been the little moments that made up our life all along.

How my life or thoughts intersect...

Wish Collisions

The pursuit of truth and beauty is a sphere of activity in which we are permitted to remain children all our lives.

~ Albert Einstein

Winter

In the distance, I see young men charging around in the exhausting activity of what appears to be some kind of extreme soccer practice.

A spry lone woman I have never seen here before who is perhaps 75 or 80 years old, passes by a block from here in front of the schoolyard. She just gotten off of the bus and wears a long, elegant emerald green coat and a clear plastic cover over perfectly coiffed white hair.

She appears fit and focused as she walks and it doesn't look like she notices the quick young athletes any more than they notice her.

Slowly, the real image fades and I picture the woman and the youthful athletes stopping in their tracks, looking at each other and becoming aware the other is there. In my mind, a sweating soccer player greets the elderly woman and they start swapping stories as each begins to truly experience what the other culture within a culture is like.

I picture the soccer players seeing great depth in the life of the elderly lady, and finding a new kind of respect for people her age as they begin to appreciate the pure beauty of old hands that once felt the essence of youth pounding through muscle and bone; they have not purchased the commercial lie that only youth is valuable and after really seeing her, listening to her, they don't believe that aging means evaporating into invisibility and uselessness.

And I imagine the elderly woman would then see the promise and excitement of youth and seek to truly understand the tremendous pressure and challenge of growing to adulthood in the world as it is today; that she would not see them as selfish, frightening beings more comfortable with electronic devices than humans and she would not dislike them for acting as others do in the era that reared them—as she probably did in the era she grew up in, too.

If these two worlds collided like that, one could shine into the other new kinds of understanding as each brings their own unique insights to the table. There would be a lot of strength in that.

The young men continue to play in the soccer field as the elderly woman walks out of view, and I wish the whole thing weren't so unlikely.

Seems people who smile broadly and ask how someone is doing are usually salespeople or greeters at restaurants or stores, unless they're related. Sad, that unless someone has something to gain from connection with another human beings, we *generally* connect with people we ourselves are most *like*.

Sitting here all these years I'm challenged to knock that off, being reminded in a fresh, new way today that everyone has something to teach whether anyone cares to learn it or not.

How my life or thoughts intersect…

For the Money

Life is what we make it, always has been,
always will be.

~ Grandma Moses

Early Autumn

Fall has arrived. Endings and new beginnings are everywhere.

The intersection is busy with cars, busses and bicycles stirring up dead leaves that chase and swirl around passengers facing a journey's beginning or end, too.

Three prim, fit women with graying hair and large handbags walk briskly along in tennis shoes and stylish, colorful windbreakers as though, like the leaves, they are pulled along and energized by the cool crisp air.

A large freight truck billboards something called the *Fine Art of Hair Care*—whatever that could be—as it moves along. As it putters by I try to imagine that fine art, *wash, scrub, rinse, condition, rinse, dry, snip, stare, snip, snip* and viola! Hair on a head is now the shape of a Grecian urn.

Or is this artistry the kind that hangs on the wall of a doctor's office, tavern or the hallway of a school?

Perhaps it's more like something seen in a museum—like one of Picasso's portraits of a human face rearranged all wacky.

Either way, someone put a lot of time, effort, money and their own kind of artistry into the creation of that huge sign on that truck.

Here comes another.

A bus is sponsored by a business that has chosen to feature a scantily clad woman who is pouting and staring anxiously at the world from the side of the bus, but I can't see from this ad just why she's doing this. Here comes another rolling advertisement touting the virtues of two mad-looking disc jockeys at a local radio station.

More buses with more ads, a van here and there with enormous logos and trucks with more colorful announcements continue to pass by either directly in front of me here at the intersection or several blocks away where they will probably connect with businesses down the street.

It's done for the money.

Somewhere, at some time, someone noticed the big blank spaces on these vehicles passing by without big photos of pouting people and fine hair art and thought, *Now that's an awful waste of prime advertising space* and, *there's a need for big pictures of people wishing they had some product they don't currently have.*

They think we humans see something like a product or a politician with a great advertising campaign and bank on the fact that a lot of us will eventually buy into what that ad is saying. Having worked in advertising, I believe the goal of any ad anywhere is simply to tell you to *open your wallet, take out a credit card or some cash and give it to us for this thing we made as cheaply as we possibly could.*

Those ads are also saying, *this thing is going to cost a lot more than an unadvertised thing because we had to pay a lot of money for this ad.*

When we buy what we buy based solely on advertising we are behaving in the advertiser's best interest, not our own, but if we suddenly stopped buying all of the overpriced silly things we buy, businesses would fold, jobs would dry up, people would go hungry and then where would we be?

These vehicles with the ads adhered to their sides are like big rolling monuments to all the hard-working people who have to slog off to the office or the high rise or the rock quarry to earn a living every day. It's hard to go to a job that kills your back and steals your time; or get up every morning to face work you have to act like you love when you hate everything but the coffee breaks (if they even let you take them).

It's difficult to be middle-aged and forced to work for a boss who is the same age as your youngest child.

Like those rigs, sometimes we working folk have to advertise something on the outside that just might not really be there at all, but we have to survive, we have to pay the bills, so doing something seemingly just for the money, isn't just for the money at all—it's much, much more.

Some can look at all they purchase with their precious time and it feels good.

It feels worth it.

But if a person is not able to find any value or reward in the work they do beyond the gathering of dollar bills, it's likely no amount of money will ever feel like enough.

Like the swirling leaves of fall that have done their job in summer and now get to separate from the tree and fly into the wind, sometimes it's the ending, that autumn-like feeling alone that will spur us on to let go and seek a brand new beginning.

How my life or thoughts intersect...

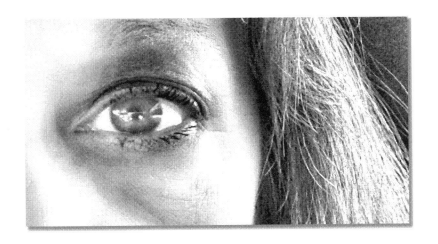

Hidden

To live remains an art which everyone must learn,
and which no one can teach.

~Havelock Ellis

Spring

So many walking by shrouded and locked up tight. I wish I knew their stories. All of them with experiences, amazing thoughts, or angry opinions, generous hearts or selfish desire all filled with memories and thoughts the world may never know.

Hidden treasure.

Yet it's rare glimpses of the fragile, brilliant once-in-a-while's that keep drawing me back even when many seasons have come and gone between visits, like today. Coming here is like coming out to play or finding something precious in my own back yard. Just walking in I start to think differently, feeling grateful for inspiring fragments and the new perspective gained by trying to see life through another person's eyes, instead of being so laser-focused on my own.

Right now I'm sitting, sipping and thinking… primarily about secrets and buried treasure.

Just watching life go by outside it occurs to me that almost from birth we are usually taught to hide unique thoughts or what makes us different out of a fear that others won't think we're normal. But after coming here for these past years I don't believe I know what the word *normal* even means.

Take what I'm doing here for example.

I've intermittently wandered into this place to sit down and write about things seen in and around the same window and intersection for over eleven years. The world might say there's nothing normal about that, but even so, it's normal for me.

Normal is different for every single one of us because like art, *normal* is both subjective and relative.

We all have our own idea of what it is, but every day we are faced with the pressure to tweak that view and learn how to best fit in. We don't want to look too foolish being who we are and as a result, feel some unnamed pressure to get certain kinds of floors, countertops, jackets, purses, shoes, cars and other products that will give us the ultimate peace of, *whew*, being normal.

Then there are all the other factors that pull and push us to get our bodies to look a certain way, our kids to achieve certain things, our hopes and dreams to all line up in the group-think land of Normal Town. We're all individuals with individual tastes, right?

So doesn't that mean in order to act or look *normal,* a person has to hide whole pieces of who they really are?

Seems to me, *normal* doesn't exist but a lot of us try to act like it does. When we do, what we end up with is a showy kind of *look at me* not *being the distinctive, delightful weirdo I really am* kind of life.

Ever notice in remembering almost any group gathering everyone else sort of blends in together, but the one who feels free to be himself enough to risk looking like a weirdo is the one easiest to remember?

How my life or thoughts intersect…

Now

The trouble with the rat race is that
even if you win you're still a rat.
~ Lilly Tomlin

Autumn

Across the way, as would-be football stars collide and shout at practice, nearby stores have Halloween decorations displayed and the painting of the strong-jawed furniture mover is still prominent in the window of the furniture store after all this time.

I wonder if the owners of the old furniture store are worried about this.

Are they in a state of panic over the fact that their store stands empty as it has for so many seasons?

Whatever they're doing, I hope they're somewhere enjoying their own little pieces of now. I'm not sure how long, but I know it's been well over a year since my last visit. It's wonderful to be back, sitting here with my coffee and open journal, looking at my favorite corner again.

Right now, there is a man in jogging shorts running past my window as if the stopwatch he clutches is actually counting the beats left in his heart. His face broadcasts agony, fierce determination or possibly both.

Maybe he's running to earn a little more time; torturing himself to thwack the odds, to beat a family history of diabetes, congestive heart failure or if—

...I look up from my journal just in time to see the running man stop six inches short of running full speed into the broad side of a moving bus. Here I am, with adrenaline about to explode out of my eyes and this guy doesn't seem to be affected at all.

He just brushes it off and keeps running. He zooms around the far corner as I shakily take a sip of coffee and stare off into the distance.

Just brush it off and keep on running. I like that.

I really like that.

Here comes another runner—a large-boned woman in an itchy-looking business suit and bright, new, white athletic shoes, awkwardly trotting at walking speed past the window with a bag of lunch in one hand and uncomfortable-looking high heels in the other.

Man, she looks miserable.

What this running woman and the running-into-the-bus man are doing inspires me on a couple levels, but the most significant is a reminder that we all operate at our own speed.

We're free to develop and find our own pace in our own kind of race in our kind of way. Sometimes we have to try a few before we discover the one that fits just right.

When we're out of step with the person we're meant to be, seems to me it shows itself in all sorts of ways like being grumpy, worn out, bored, stressed or depressed and that's the stuff that can lead to all sorts of ways to self-medicate and all sorts of ways to push everything even farther away.

A taxicab stops at the intersection as if on cue filled with a couple more examples of this.

The driver looks sleepy and leans in on the steering wheel, which appears to be holding him upright—his connection to it reminds me of the runner's stopwatch—as if it's somehow tied to his ability to sit up and breathe.

He doesn't look happy. In fact, in the brief time he's at the intersection I can clearly see this guy is half-asleep and beyond bored, more like on the verge of a coma.

Next, a car with a large magnetic sign affixed to the side saying *Student Driver* pulls up right after the weary cab driver.

The look on the face of the teacher, the Expert Driver, is almost the same as the cabbie, as if each ho-hum-hum-hum routine is wearing both completely through.

Can't imagine how frightening these two jobs could be.

One, driving complete strangers around who could be insane and/or packing heat, the other voluntarily giving young people who were just in infant car seats a decade-plus ago control over his life. Each driver's workday could potentially be peppered with terrifying, brake-stomping, dashboard-clawing moments in heavy traffic, hour after hour with a continual flow of strangers and criminals or inexperienced, legally-a-child drivers behind the wheel.

Both sound trying and extremely difficult to face day after day, but neither sounds boring.

The teacher and student pull up and pause for longer than usual at the intersection after the cab pulls away.

The look on the face of the student driver is one of anticipation and excitement, it is the expression of one embarked on a thrilling new beginning. I can see her bright eyes from here. The contrast between the faces of teacher and student is like that between a puppy with a brand new squeaky toy and an old dog annoyed by a fleabite he can't reach.

156

These people are in the same airspace, at the same intersection, and essentially doing the same thing and the only differences—at least from my limited viewpoint in this place and time—are the individuals and their experience levels and attitudes.

We've each been dealt a certain number of given cards but experience and attitude are two cards we have some control over.

Experience and attitude.

They have tremendous power to influence all that we are or ever hope to become. They determine our racing direction, speed and where and how we finish. They will fight off boredom, complacency, and will help us avoid potholes and help us stay in the race even when we feel like quitting.

Experience and attitude do this because along the way, if we listen to our lives, we discover how powerful it is to keep on running when we make a mistake or wrong turn.

And just like the runners earlier, you and I and these drivers are all free to find our own pace and run our own race using our own life experiences and attitude to fuel us and help keep us moving.

The neat thing is, while we're all in the race we don't race against each other, we race to be our very best ME, because in the end, the only one we've ever really raced against is ourselves.

How my life or thoughts intersect...

Butcher Paper

When everything seems to be going against you, remember that the airplane takes off against the wind, not with it.

~ Henry Ford

Winter

It's cold out today and the sky is dark and ominous as if the sun never rose. Fierce clouds pour frigid rain into the atmosphere threatening to harden into a glaze of ice.

Not much movement outside today, what with rain slicing down in icy machine-gun pellets blown sideways by the wind.

Won't stay long. I'll just sit a moment, have some hot coffee and be on my way.

How often do entire seasons pass between visits?

The furniture store no longer has the smiling mover painted on the window. It feels like he was looking out over Jackson and Main since the beginning. I wonder now when his image disappeared and who had the job of removing him.

It would be nice to think Happy Moving Guy left on his own, joyfully carrying home appliances into sales-land oblivion.

If I shut my eyes I can still see him—in his sweet cartoonish way—taking every last item off to some ecstatic cartoon customer who deeply appreciates his efforts.

Pretty sure the cartoon people tip him well, too.

The store must have finally been sold since butcher paper covers the windows now. If the paper is there to keep the world from seeing inside, it's working. Still, the fact that it's there makes me wonder what they don't want us to see.

Is the paper there to keep sunlight from fading new carpet and amazing new products or to keep potential thieves from considering how easy it might be to just tap that glass and with a *tink* and a crash, make off with some of that old furniture?

Maybe someone took the trouble to cover all those huge picture windows because no one is home and there are no new prospects in sight. Perhaps the neighborhood store still houses out-of-date furniture that's become obsolete because consumers tend to grow weary of familiar things they used to clamor for.

Maybe there are people inside the old furniture store who are busy painting and getting ready to open the place again with some exciting new venture and they don't want us to know what they're up to in there.

I wonder.

Suddenly, the sidewalk and intersection are bustling.

People appear out of nowhere, braving the elements in order to get out of the nasty weather and head to destinations less damp and glacial than this corner. Some look relaxed, as if heading home but most are collected, cold and focused, ready to get into someplace warmer than here.

If any of the chilly ones who have just scurried out from buildings to catch buses—or those in automobiles stopping and driving by—are concerned with the secret goings-on inside an old has-been furniture store it doesn't show.

When it's cold and unpleasant outside, most of us do the bare minimum while exposed to it.

Seems to be the same with people. When human lives, like windows are covered and there is no way to see in, we gradually lose interest and cease to even try looking in.

How my life or thoughts intersect...

It's Working

It is while you are patiently toiling at the little tasks of life
that the meaning and shape
of the great whole of life dawn on you.

~ Phillips Brooks

Summer

Right now, just outside my window, three painters in the summer sun, are tearing down a scaffold they were just using.

They work together with no words exchanged between them as if they have done this so many times the routine is automatic.

They work quickly and efficiently.

One man wears a sweatshirt that reads, *Just Paint It.*

He knows his job and he is doing it well. In fact, in the short time it has taken me to write this, the entire, one-story tall scaffold has been put completely away. All three men did their work without any visible complaining and without using any excess verbiage, and the job was done in a fast and efficient manner.

I'm sitting here thinking, *Man, that didn't look like much fun.*

Their actions looked almost robotic, but who's to say whether they were having a good time or not?

We're all wired so differently and see things so differently it's a miracle any of us ever gets along with any of the rest of us.

These guys weren't slapping each other on the back, giving the big high fives or goofing around, but I have to remember that some people truly enjoy the simple act of doing a job efficiently and don't have to laugh out loud or shoot off sky flares to prove it.

They could be different people when they're at home or out with family and friends.

I know I miss seeing the whole picture here—just given casual hints at what may lie beneath.

There's no way to tell the real heart of a person, particularly just watching them at work…

…because what we do is not what or who we are.

How my life or thoughts intersect...

<u>What Matters?</u>

Relationships.
People.
Who we become.
> *...that's what matters.*

Everything else fades as
> *Now churns into*
Tomorrow and Tomorrow and Tomorrow
> *adding up and spilling into eternity.*

Every person negotiates his pathway in the way that seems best
at the time,

using tools and road maps found along the way,
　　using the challenges given before and after he's born
added to the good and bad choices he makes and what he
allows to grow on the inside
and poof,
　　　　there's a lifetime.

We are each our own unique story.
A story of
Trying to understand another,
Trying to see who's beneath damage hidden under our
bandage-masks can be like
looking through dark, deep water,
　　flying sightless in thick fog,
　　or trying to see in through venetian blinds broken shut.

Each mask twisting, skewing how we see
　　ourselves and
　　　　the rest of the world.

Once we decide to seek to understand each other and put away
automatic self-defenses
　　respect begins to grow.

　　Pieces of truth start falling into place and the puzzle
becomes more complete.

All the temporary, outer-image trappings, become less and less
important.
　　Masks begin to crumble,
　　　　leaving honesty and relationship where
fear and isolation once were.

All that really matters
Is
What comes with us when
We're done.

We are part of a living symphony
one in which
notes can change
and songs may be rewritten.

The sound becomes a sharing thing that resonates to the world
through the unique being
you call me
and when that me
discovers the ignition of grace
in all its glory
that me is able to extend real love,

Life on Earth exists
in the music made together
because those are the songs
that never fade.

How my life or thoughts intersect...

The Spark

Pleasure is very seldom found where it is sought.
Our brightest blazes are commonly kindled by
unexpected sparks.

~ Samuel Johnson

Early Spring

Springtime has arrived again on Jackson and Main.

The cherry blossoms are still intently clinging to their host branches. Only a few have let go and flown full into the wind.

A spring rain has washed the scene with a refreshing thunder of clean. And those birds that move as if they are connected—the kind that fly in formation like a huge blanket—are flying and flowing through the windy schoolyard in a silent, swirling celebration of the changing seasons.

A little pert woman in a stylish peach-colored coat clutches her purchase and peers into the window as if this were one-way glass. She doesn't focus on me, so she can't see me, even though I'm just a foot from her face.

It's a menu she seeks. Wants to see the menu before she commits herself to opening the door, I suppose.

We only really see what we focus on.

A man with a heavy load of schoolbooks in his arms paces nervously at the bus stop. He's not a boy. He is a grown man who doesn't appear to have lost the fire, the questions, or the desire to learn. I love to see that spark, that light that wonders how, and wonders why. He looks at his watch, clearly filled with anticipation.

Like the new growth of springtime all around, love of learning grows if cultivated and encouraged. I wonder if a special someone cheers him on, or if it comes from within.

Either way, he wins.

How my life or thoughts intersect...

Parking and People

A straight oar looks bent in the water.
What matters is not merely that we see things
but how we see them.

~ Michel de Montaigne

Summer

A man in the brightest neon orange jacket I have ever seen writes a letter, a love sonnet or a lengthy ticket to someone who abuses a parking privilege.

Pretty sure it's a ticket.

You would think the bearer of bad news would not wish to stick out like a giant, Macy's Thanksgiving Day Parade balloon, wafting down the street in his glowing, attention-demanding jacket. You'd think he'd just do his work and try to skulk away unnoticed, until the criminal who parks incorrectly returns and grimaces with a *now-that-just-makes-my-day* kind of look.

His has to be a tough job.

Who's happy to see him writing up a ticket except a few business owners? I'll bet that's hard to take day in and day out.

Watching him place a ticket on a windshield, for some reason I imagine his first day of work as someone behind a counter with a clipboard hands him the gaudy orange garment.

In my daydream, I see his right eye begin to twitch slightly as he puts one arm in the thing, then the other, the whole time feeling like he did back in 5th grade on safety patrol.

He moves on down the block in search of another vehicle guilty of breaking the law.

It's a beautiful summer afternoon on Jackson and Main.

The American flag snaps smartly in the breeze by City Hall; a teenager uses the pay phone just outside the window and speaks in an animated fashion while tossing her head around and slapping her thigh.

A man in sunglasses and black leather jacket gets comfortable in the shady grass near the bus stop. A determined-looking woman in a mustard-yellow pantsuit hurries past the window with little twin black-haired boys as they bounce in the general direction of the school.

Here come two middle-aged people walking down the sidewalk with signs. One is a dark-haired man in a black business suit and the other, a fast-talking heavy-set, jean-clad blonde woman. As the two quickly pass my window I can't quite tell if the signs they carry are for a garage sale or if they are political signs to hammer into lawns.

On different scales, the end result of either probably has a lot of similarities.

Just this second I notice a sign I've never seen before, but by the looks of it, it's been there a long time. They must have trimmed the trees last fall.

Across the street, past the branches of the budding cherry tree, on the long-empty furniture store, there, above the place where the smiling moving man picture used to be, above the awning, up near the roof, is a huge sign on display saying, *Happy Holidays, Have a great new year. Welcome to our town.*

Wow.

Why would the creators of this sign think and scheme and budget and pay for such a huge bit of information that is so difficult to see?

How did I miss it all this time? I come into this little restaurant with the sole purpose of noticing things and after all these years have passed—even since the furniture store closed—I finally see it.

Has anyone else on the planet, aside from the people who decided to put it there, ever even *looked* at it?

Perhaps this sign is like so many other sentiments in advertising that burble out to the world as just a sputtering of *polite* that has no real heart.

I'd like to think the creator of that sign really wanted me to have a nice holiday and a great new year, but I kinda doubt it.

Taking a sip of hot coffee and looking again at the huge billboard-ish Christmas card overlooking the intersection, I wonder how many other signs are nearby and so obvious I never really see them at all.

How my life or thoughts intersect...

Love's Winter Sky

The world breaks everyone,
but afterward,
some are strong at the broken places.

~ Ernest Hemingway

Winter

Each of us live our own story in a book written by our choices and decisions and it takes place between the pages of ordinary, normal, every-day days—just like today. As I sit here drinking in the changing seasons, those life-scenes continue to unfold as a series of wonderful, unending stories.

Turning from the window, I see a 70-something man at the register.

He buys a cup of coffee, carries it in one hand and walks my way with tattered paper bag and newspaper tucked under his arm—he looks familiar. Sitting down at the table next to me, he says hello and, *Hey, didn't I see you about an hour ago in that little thrift store two blocks down?*

I tell him *Yes, I found some pretty good books there.*

He tells me the money goes to a good cause, that's why he likes shopping there for little trinkets and such.

We talk about the store and he says he just needed a cup of coffee and a little rest before walking home.

We exchange pleasantries, says his friends call him Bud. I tell him my friends call me Lindy. He sips his coffee, discovers it's too hot and sets it down again.

You'll have to forgive me, he says with weary eyes, *I seem to just start talkin' to people sometimes.*

I tell him I don't mind because it's nice to know friendly people still exist in the world. He smiles half a smile saying how no one wants to listen to him so much anymore it seems, *my kids live close but they're busy,* he says, *most of my friends have moved away or are gone now, and my Alice, my wife of 46 years died just a handful of months ago and...* he stops, lifting his gaze to the window as if he can see something there that I cannot and stops.

The silence slows time as I awkwardly try not to intrude on his sorrowful retreat. After a little while he continues...*and it's just awful hard to go on without her.* He slowly looks down into the steaming black liquid inside his coffee cup.

I'm so sorry for your loss, I say, realizing as I say it how empty and hollow it sounds. All I have to offer this man is a willingness to listen. He is silent for a while, collecting himself. *I'm sorry for going on like that,* he says. I tell him I don't mind. A wave of gratitude washes over his face as he smiles; *She was my best friend, my sweetheart.*

He takes a worn handkerchief out of his pocket and wipes his eyes, *...my Alice.*

He turns away and says *I'm sorry, so sorry,* he says.

I tell him there's no reason to apologize, that she must have been someone special and ask what she was like.

A subtle, warm change comes over his face as he begins to speak of her and their life together. His posture changes and his eyes brighten as he describes how they met, how she loved to garden and sew and oh, how he loved her.

194

The dark hue of loss lifts enough to show a glimmer of the mural that was their life together.

There is a particular kind of poetry in the heart and soul of those who have loved well, and loved long. This man shares the story of his life with Alice as easily as snowflakes falling from a winter sky.

Holding up the folded newspaper he says, *Every day she walked down our long driveway to get the paper so I'd have it with my coffee.*

He gingerly sips his hot coffee, picks up the paper and continues, *I, well, I guess I didn't appreciate it much then, but now I walk about a mile and a half from home to the store past the corner to get it, thinkin' of her and all those little things she used to do the whole way.*

Bud sighs and stands, leaves half a cup of coffee and gathers his things to leave. *Looks like we got some cold comin' in,* he says, *better get headed for home.*

As he walks past my chair I tell him I wish I could have met her, she sounds like a wonderful lady. He stops by my chair, leans down grins brightly and warmly pats my hand. *That she was,* he says nodding, *that she surely was.*

I ask if he would like a ride, but he shakes his head no, pauses by the door a moment and turning back says, *But thanks. Y'know, most folks don't know what to do or say. Some say move on, some give advice. Almost no one wants to listen and most of 'em, even our kids, just leave me alone, I 'preciate you listening. Means a lot.*

Bud wipes a work-worn hand through gray hair and shuffles out the door.

I watch him make his way up the hill, and he looks like everyone, all of us, tender complexities in fragile, human packages, sooner or later facing deep loss. But what a privilege it is to love and be loved so deeply. That kind of loss becomes celebration after the raw pain heals over.

That kind of love truly never dies.

Perhaps Bud was able to smile so brightly between the tears because loving someone with all of his heart caused an awful lot of good to grow, and that brings in lovelies that never leave even when you can't see them anymore.

How my life or thoughts intersect...

Us and Ours

"Sometimes the questions are complicated and the answers are simple."

~ *Dr. Seuss*

Spring

My journal is open and a fresh cup of coffee steams in front of me as I settle in and get comfortable again here at my window.

Thinking comes easy here because outside that window there are a million distractions and all the rest of my life to deal with. Out there I have a never-ending to-do list constantly reproducing itself almost every moment of every day.

Being here teaches me things I couldn't possibly learn cocooned inside busyness and noise and helps me return to my day-to-day life out there with a little more understanding.

A bus grumbles as it exits and pulls away from the stop. No one arrives and no one departs.

The street outside remains uncharacteristically empty and the silence in the café is broken by voices of two women talking behind me. I can't see them, but one asks the other if she knows about the sale for 25% off at the local Big Store.

The other woman must be looking at her organizer to write down the sale because she reminds her friend that today is Good Friday. They chat about how fast Easter has crept up this year and laugh when one says it's a good thing they don't go to church or they'd have to buy something dressy to wear.

Good Friday.

For some reason the thought of it reminds me of a frosty night many years ago on the farm I grew up on, when my dad decided to teach my sister Shirley and me the Lord's Prayer.

Pop sat between our beds as I snuggled down, my feet warming on the towel-wrapped canning jar filled with hot water that Mom had placed under the pile of handmade quilts to chase some of the winter cold away.

He tells us it's important to know this particular prayer because Jesus told some folks it was the best way to talk to God. Said it was pretty important to learn. Pop repeated a part of a phrase and Shirley and I would say it back to him, but first he said the entire thing, most of which I didn't understand, especially the part about what I thought was *detts* and *detters*.

Our Father, it begins. The first word of the most important prayer starts with *Our*.

Today is Good Friday.

Today I think about Easter dresses, friends, burdens, crosses to bear and the fact that an awful lot of us walk around disconnected with the rest of the world—as if no one else matters. Picturing Pop's jet-black hair and strong face in the dim light of a winter's night as our instruction of *an important thing to learn* continues, but today I'm stuck on those first two words. *Our Father.*

Not *My*, not *Mine*. *Ours*.

Life isn't an *Us* against *Them* kind of deal. It's *Us*. It's an *Us* and *Ours* kind of deal.

No matter how different we look, think, feel, react, speak or act, we may irritate and aggravate each other, we may not understand each other and some may never even begin to try, but the fact is, this life is no solitary work because one way or another this life is about *Us*.

I think of Good Friday and burdens to bear, how we all have had, still have or will have massive crosses to carry; weighty, harsh things that devastate and bend us low, causing hearts to break and lives to change.

A lot of us learn at an early age to hide damage and how we feel inside, so the darkest stuff is invisible; so we won't look or act in such a way that would make someone else uncomfortable. We're expected to put the big things, the huge crosses away and not bother the world with them, because being completely honest makes a lot of people want to run screaming from the room.

We learn along our road that expressing emotions like full-throttle sorrow, rage, fear, delight, passion, laughter or disgust are seen as being out of control, selfish, weak and lacking in class. Self-control is an admirable thing, but how often do we take it too far and are simply dishonest?

Because any display of emotion causes a few to blink hard and draw back, fakery keeps the status quo in place because who needs more weight added to their own?

Yet especially today it becomes more and more obvious that we're all connected and part of something much bigger than the *just me*.

Here, self-focused smallness fades as lives intersect with others, painting the world in individual, bright swaths of unique colors blending together, creating breathtaking hues more wondrous than can ever be seen through the life of one alone. As I look outside on this this Good Friday, each person passing by the window seems to repeat the theme *we aren't alone*. We all carry burdens and have our own crosses of varying sizes to haul along whether or not those crosses will ever be seen.

The biggest burdens are usually those that hit us out of left field and leave us out of control—because in reality, we *are* at a loss and our entire world *is* out of control. I've come to realize the one thing I have control over in life is the Me I choose to become by the finish line.

On Good Friday I think of a walk made long ago by one so filled with the deepest kind of other-love that he chose to wipe away stone-cold death by giving his life—for us.

I remember reading the story, picturing Jesus falling to the earth alone, unable to carry his cross, the massive, awful instrument of his death. As he falls, a stranger from the crowd is told to pick up the huge wooden cross and drag it to the place where Christ will die.

This Good Friday I think about the fact that since the Son of God didn't carry his burden alone, why do I think I can?

Burdens.

Yours, mine, us, ours.

As the street outside continues to fill with life, people rush past all the rest who are busy living within their own private story. We've all walked and waded through a lot to get to this today. Who out there is bursting with something wonderful to share, a deep question, a fear, a huge success just waiting to be told?

Who is bored with life or feels she has no reason to get up again?

Who just wants to survive and make it through another day?

Whose hearts breaks within lives completely shattered by painful messages sent inside small pieces; one sentence uttered low by a somber doctor, a terrifying phone call, a long, sad look leading to a short and final good-bye?

Us. Ours.

Looking out this window on Good Friday, I see it's still an imperfect world filled with imperfect people doing imperfect things, but today it's a place filled with <u>Us</u>, not just me and not just you. And here we all are, trying to make it through another day.

Some days we get by just fine, but the times when we say and do the selfish, wrong or hurtful things we all at some point, say and do, Good Friday comes along and reminds that there's another way to handle things that frankly, doesn't hurt so much. The one way that says we never again have to face another day without another heart to share it with.

God so loved the world that he gave...

For us.

How my life or thoughts intersect...

Birds and Bitterness

He lives long that lives well;
and time misspent is not lived, but lost.

~ Thomas Fuller

Winter

Friends don't walk like that.

A woman and a man walk together, yet at an obviously angry distance. They are side-by-side but walk far apart with dark emotions distorting their faces.

Looking past the fury it dawns on me, *I know her from a group event and that man is her husband.*

His face is downcast and full of rage. Her gaze is desperate, angry and fixed as they walk, not speaking, both with jaw and hands clenched.

This looks like titanic chasms of disconnect reaching far beyond the result of some simple argument; emotions so overwhelming they carry them and dictate how they walk, where they walk, how they look and possibly how they see.

I wonder when this began.

When did they meet?

Were they young and both innocent and amazed?

Did time, trials and differences sift away that first sweet infatuation with a thousand little hurtful things carving anger and disgust where trust, dreams and dignity were meant to grow?

We humans are all so different, all so alien to each other, that to find any two who actually get along for long periods of time is impossible unless those two are willing to work, work, work at it and refuse to ever give up.

We all have loose screws, you and I, just like this man and this woman.

None of us on this planet of ours can ever completely understand someone else because we usually try to figure each other out based on our own unique binoculars—when no one else on the planet has binoculars like our own.

These two dear people are unable to see what the other sees right now and right now, it appears they have lost the will to even try.

They walk past the window just as a blackbird flits from tree to puddle and sits in the middle of the busy intersection.

He lifts one wing and pecks at himself, oddly oblivious to the danger of vehicles rushing past, inches away.

As the blackbird begins to splash about in the dirty, oil-stained puddle I see a connection between his actions and the couple passing by.

Even in the midst of chaos and company, we are each in the end, alone. What we do with that aloneness and what happens inside of that aloneness holds rewards as well as consequences.

It takes so little to just look up and be aware, to pay attention and offer people we love simple things like respect and appreciation. Massive consequences are at stake because it's the little things we ignore that can become big things that merge to sweep it all away.

Maybe the blackbird becomes careless and unafraid because he's focused solely on himself.

Who alive hasn't done that?

Who knows, maybe the man and the woman are self-protecting and do that, too. Whatever it is, at least today, by all appearances, something caused the sweet sound of the other's voice to become the droning beat of an enemy drum.

When sweet nothings are transformed into hurtful little somethings they add up, too.

I learn again and again here that our lives are made up of little things, and like pennies or bits of garbage tossed in a jar, they accumulate. Little things *do* add up.

All of them.

Good or bad. Love or hate. Hurtful or healing.

Whatever we allow to be tossed into our jar adds up and sooner or later, the jar gets full.

The question is, what do we want to have in the end when we empty it out, because we're the ones who decide what goes in to begin with.

How my life or thoughts intersect...

What We Can't See

Things do not pass for what they are,
but for what they seem.
Most things are judged by their jackets.

Baltasar Gracian

Spring

Firemen in uniform red t-shirts walk and run around their shiny clean fire engine. The truck is back from some unknown location—a house fire, a medical concern, a feline rescue or some such fireman business.

It is parked outside with emergency flashers on, and the whole thing looks like some kind of exciting celebration.

A man glides past the window with huge Paul Bunyan-like strides as his wild blonde hair floats slowly up and down.

His arms are full of big, elegant, cream-white business envelopes. These are serious, formal-looking envelopes, quite unlike their messenger, who reaches up with one hand and whisks an untamed lock of hair out of his eyes. It floats back out of place as he continues on without stopping.

In one fluid movement, he crosses the street, opens the mailbox and *whoosh*, deposits his armload inside and turns to walk back again.

The relaxed, easy-going style of the messenger doesn't match those envelopes.

He has a casual appearance and I'll bet he's either the boss in charge or someone like a mailroom assistant. Both have little to lose by being relaxed and comfortable in their work.

At any other level, the messenger might dress more like the envelopes themselves, all suited up.

At the same time, the firemen continue working diligently, cleaning and polishing the last few inches of the newly washed fire engine.

It looks so nice it could be in a public service announcement or a children's storybook about the friendly neighborhood fire truck named Freddy or something.

I picture a fireman and the messenger standing side-by-side and wonder if most of us would automatically trust one more than the other based solely on their jobs or how they dress.

Appearances.

Either way, both the firemen and the messenger drink in the sunshine, enjoying their careers today.

The woman behind the counter here is definitely not enjoying hers. I don't know what she's struggling with, or why she's behaving like she is, but she makes no pretense at being even remotely pleasant. Her anger is palpable, and I actually wish, for the first time, that I had not come in.

She furrows her brow, grimaces and questions my order when I ask for both coffee and soda with my lunch.

It's odd to feel unwelcome here, but I remind myself by reading what I'd just written earlier, that appearances are deceiving. Sometimes, when we're overwhelmed, we human beings just retreat into caged animal stance, not even knowing that doing so just makes everything worse.

Even so, trying to understand why she behaves like she does doesn't make her rudeness any easier to stomach.

Everyone acts like a jerk once in a while for any number of reasons, but I've never met anyone who likes to be around when the being-a-jerk attack hits. I order my lunch and return to my window seat, glad to be done dealing with her.

Trying to think about something else, I look outside and see a truck that has a huge pink sign explaining the fine job this company does cleaning toilets.

Someone hatched an idea to do this and formed a business with that toilet-cleaning idea in mind. Meetings were probably held on the color scheme, the logo, the catchy name, and this promotion plan.

I can see them discuss the latest toilet-cleaning products, chemicals and brushes in great depth, and with lots of energy as they write on big charts and graphs. It's clear someone put a lot of effort into having a cute, pretty sign so people don't look at what they do and think, *oh...ew-w.*

A photo of a dirty toilet probably wouldn't bring in too many eager customers.

Appearances. Again.

I guess I think about that a lot. And just as I'm thinking that I think about it a lot, something else happens that makes me think about it even more.

While sitting here sipping my coffee and soda I hear the voice of a tiny, sweet little girl behind me. She sounds as if she can't be older than two, but she must be extremely verbal for her age. I turn to look at the child and a very tall, very large redheaded woman in a purple velour sweat suit, who must be the mom, blocks my view.

After a time, I sense the child behind me has gotten up and is over near the cash register, asking about things in the display case and interested in the ice cream machine. I can't see her, but she is possibly the most polite little girl I've ever heard.

I quickly glance back to get a glimpse of her, and again the woman in the purple velour blocks my view of the sweet child.

The woman behind the counter is even nastier to the mother and preschooler than she was to me; I don't understand because the little girl is so polite when she asks for the least expensive ice cream, *just one small scoop in a dish, please.*

I turn again to see if I can see her and at first cannot believe my eyes.

There is no child.

The sizeable woman wearing purple velour is alone.

The tiny voice is hers.

After the cone is made, she reminds the waitress that she cannot afford a cone, and asks again, just as sweetly, for her ice cream in a dish because it's less expensive.

The woman behind the counter takes the cone and slams it upside down it in a dish, brusquely slamming it down on the counter in front of the woman in purple barking, *Won't charge for cone, just dish of ice cream, then!*

This doesn't seem to faze the woman in purple.

She thanks the volatile server, taking quarters, dimes and pennies out of her coin purse, counts them out into the outstretched hand of the woman behind the counter and sits down to enjoy her desert as the angry clerk storms back to the cash register.

After eating her ice cream, she gets up to leave, clears her table and wipes it down. On her way out, she tells someone sitting near the door to have a great day and then walks out the door.

I bus my table, pick up my things and get up and run after her.

By the time I catch up, she is a block away, sitting at the bus stop by the school and I have absolutely no idea what I'm doing there or what to say or do next.

Quite a few people are waiting for the next bus and there I stand, looking goofy and nervous like I'm at my first dance.

After loitering around a few moments making things even more awkward, I square my shoulders and just walk up to her and say hello.

She looks up, smiles and returns my greeting. I fumble around in my purse a few seconds because I still don't know what I'm doing and manage to mutter out, *I, uh, I was having lunch over there, and I, uh, just had to tell you that you made my day with your sweet attitude even after the woman behind the counter was so rude to you.*

I'm thinking she must be as unsure as to why I followed her over there as I am, but her smile slowly broadens.

Others at the bus stop lean in a bit to listen, a group of teenagers look at each other and one elbows a buddy in a *get a load of this* gesture, but it doesn't matter.

She leans forward, squints a little and says *Do I know you? Are you one of those ladies from that church over there?* Gesturing behind her, a slight apprehension in her voice.

No, I say, *but I have done some public speaking at some groups like writer's groups, clubs and churches—could we have met then?*

No, she says, still a little suspiciously, *I would have remembered.*

I tell her that …*I'm really not crazy. I was sitting in that café you just left and needed to let you know how much I admire your reaction to that unpleasant woman back there.*

She leans back and says *I guess she was just having a bad day.*

That had to be it, I say, *she's never been so bad-tempered before…*

Some of those gathered at the bus stop are riveted to our conversation and all are silent.

It was sweet of you to come talk to me, she smiles.

I thank her again and turn to leave as she says, *Uhm, you have really pretty hair, it looks like gold.* I smile and tell her *the color's from a box, but I appreciate the compliment.* She smiles again, and looking at her I say, *you encourage other people just by being you, you know.*

As I walk back to the crosswalk I hear her shout, *and…and you have a beautiful smile!*

We exchange waves. Walking back across the crosswalk toward the café I'm grateful for who this woman is and thankful to have met her.

Today was a peek into things we can't see, like the tremendous power inside every one of us to touch another life for good or for bad; that negative emotion spreads like a virus; but what I love most about what happened here today is seeing it's not just that negative multiplies, but respect, kindness and encouragement can be contagious, too.

How my life or thoughts intersect...

Strangers

As I grow older I pay less attention to what men say.
I just watch what they do.

~ Andrew Carnegie

Summer

It's one of the few truly beautiful summer days so far this year. We have been soaked to the skin and back by torrents of rain for so long, I've forgotten what dry pavement looks like. Flowers literally explode the landscape as a result of the sobbing, hysterical sky, but it seems they all but laugh at the contrast between this July and the drought we dry-heaved through last year.

Some folks behind me are unhappy that someone in Wisconsin won the $150 million dollar lottery. They are disgruntled and speak in harsh, loud tones.

The money should go to someone here in our own state says one.

You bet.

A stranger is still a stranger says another.

Don't need any strangers who live out of state getting what's ours.

Strangers need to just stay away from here.

…Just stay the hell away.

Hmmm. *A stranger is still a stranger.* The words hang heavy in the air like the smell of old dead fish. What exactly then, is a stranger? What makes someone who lives within the borders of this state "one of us" while someone two feet beyond it an alien? After thinking about this for quite some time, it becomes obvious what connects us. It's the things we have in common. We are all connected to the other in ways we may not always be able to see. Most of us can look at the world and see both good and bad, even if our definitions are different:

- Rain falls on all of us; the sun warms all of us, stranger or not.
- We all want to love and be loved.
- We face struggles and would like to be significant somehow.
- Our hearts can break, and we can all bleed.
- We know anger, hope, peace, and temptation and too many of us know how it feels to be cold, alone and hungry.
- We have felt fear and have laughed out loud.
- We have dreams and desires and have had our share of good days and bad.

Not one of us is a stranger in the purest sense of the word because we're connected in all that we share—because of that, we know a lot about each other. To look only at what separates us is like giving up on crossing a river when there's a bridge just beyond the next corner.

To focus solely on differences makes as much sense as choosing to look only at the back of a painting. When we choose instead, to look at all we have in common, lines of distinction fade.

Strangers are strangers only because we choose to see them that way and keep them that way

228

How my life or thoughts intersect...

The Two-by-Four

The first thing which I can record concerning myself is, that I was born.
These are wonderful words.
This life, to which neither time nor eternity can bring diminution - this everlasting living soul, began.
My mind loses itself in these depths.

~ Groucho Marx

Late Autumn

It's been years since I first saw him, and since that first time here on Jackson & Main, I've wanted to meet him face to face and tell him what an impact he has had on my life.

In all these years, I've never seen him walk in this restaurant like he did today. I don't think it's considered PC to call someone a blind person, but today I was the one who was blind, because I couldn't see him walk up past the window, come in the door, go to the counter, order, sit down or eat his lunch.

I didn't notice one single thing about him until he was out the door and I'd like to try to blame it on the kids.

An unwieldy group of junior high students filled the room with the wails and noxious noise of attitude and hormones.

Even now, more of them crowd in and fill this space, bumping my table as my teeth clench and I wonder where the angry manager is when I need her. They are shout-speaking and behave so rudely I decide I need to pack up and leave.

As I hurry up to eat the last few bites of soup it becomes more apparent that when children step out of innocence into the world of *intentional,* things begin to change.

At this age they sprint toward individuality, and being in a group out in the wild like this with no parents or teachers present, boundaries are pushed, shoved and mowed down.

They are loud and obnoxious and my anger is all I can see, and because of that, I was the loser today. Looking at the girls' thick make-up and trampy clothes it's hard to picture them as innocent little two year-olds with big bright eyes and tiny rosebud hands reaching up to be held.

The boys have baggy pants and dirty underwear exposed-on-purpose and their conversation is peppered with loud obscenities and various bodily gases being freed into this air in here.

Like I said, I was furious and getting ready to leave until The Big Thing happened and after it did, I didn't feel so blind anymore.

After it happened I could see that the *Look at me, Mom* still evolves in them, and the caterpillar struggles to break free of its cocoon and be accepted even though it does so with little thought as to how it's freedom fight might affect anyone else.

I started to stop judging them and to see these kids as people who just want to figure out who they are while not looking too dorky in the process.

After it happened, I realized it would be tough to be that age any day, but it's particularly difficult today…stumbling through the throes of puberty and adolescence, more child than adult living in a media-obsessed world as they try to deal with complex feelings like their own sexuality that just a few seasons ago, meant nothing.

234

In the midst of all this, they're expected to behave maturely when they don't even know what that is or who they are yet in these foreign, changing bodies.

It started as three of the boys try to take over the conversation with their wannabe manly ways but two of the girls talk so loudly and the exchange ends so profoundly I won't be able to forget it.

One lanky girl turns to another, slurring her words as she smacks out, *I thought Travis is, like this f------g jerk.*

Me too! Squeaks the small blonde as she adjusts an undergarment.

Lanky Girl rolls her eyes, *I thought, he's like, this total dork, but...*

Yeah? Asks Tiny Blonde with whorish make-up on little-girl eyes.

Lanky leans in, like she's telling a precious secret, *He's not, if you like, pay attention and really listen, he's not like that at all.*

I know. Tiny Blonde pops her gum as an exclamation point.

He's got, like, you know, this good, heart inside, says Lanky Girl as she fusses with a metal object in her hair.

Noisily slurping the remnants of a long-gone Pepsi as she holds her gum, Tiny says *He DOES, he is such a totally, and oh-my-gawd-TOTALLY nice guy.*

I know, right? Says Lanky, nodding like a bobble-head.

Tiny puts her gum back in her mouth and warms it up with a few good pops as she says, *People don't,* (pop) *know that about him, 'cause they just, you know, judge him before they know him.*

Judge him before they know him.

For years I've wanted to meet the man from a long time ago who had a seeing eye dog and taught about little right things without saying a word; but I was too judgmental and pissed off at the intrusive noise of children to notice that he had come in until he walked out the door.

To chase after him would have meant pushing my way through a shoulder-to-shoulder herd of preteens and he was already boarding the bus.

Now he's gone.

My God, how many moments like this have I missed?

How often do I judge before I know anything about a situation or someone because I'm focusing on what seems wrong instead of trying to understand or look for even the little things that are right?

How my life or thoughts intersect...

Childhood and Change

Love doesn't make the world go 'round.
Love is what makes the ride worthwhile.

~ Franklin P. Jones

Winter

A chilly wind whips about outside as a bus with a number that indicates it is destined for my childhood hometown pulls up to the stop.

The street is empty, but my mind boards the bus. I shut my eyes and drift away from the winter chill outside, gliding through time as the bus journeys out of the city through familiar landscapes of rich, green farmland alive with the hum of busy insects dancing midst summer blooms.

Bright sunshine strobes through tall timber as season upon season rush past and we make our way across countryside and pieces of the past.

In an instant, pavement turns to the gravel road leading up to our old red farmhouse. Cows slowly munch grass in the far field past the garden and fruit orchards; I can barely make out the distant sound of Pop's chainsaw in the thick forest behind the pasture. Three chestnut brown horses stand in the shade of the barn, flicking black tails in the heat as chickens murmur and peck in dry summer earth.

My imagination comes to a stop outside the kitchen door and I can almost smell Mom's dinner on the stove and hear the sounds of laughter, pets and family.

Abruptly, my time-machine bubble bursts as two talkative businessmen enter the restaurant opening the door to the café and ushering in a blast of icy wind.

Looking once again at the bus outside, it closes its doors and departs. Seems I was the only one to board the bus to my hometown today.

The bus leaves empty.

Outside, all is still. There are no cars at the intersection, no joggers trotting past, no students at the bus stop or shoppers walking by.

Curious. There to the right of the bus stop, all of a sudden I notice something is missing.

Something is out of place.

Something is gone.

At first, it's like looking at a friend who just shaved off his mustache. You notice a strange difference, but you don't know what it is for a while.

The expanse of grass and the shading oak trees beside the bus stop have been replaced by a cold, cement *Staff Only* parking lot.

A parking lot.

They left the big tree, but as for the rest, they took paradise and they put up a lousy, effing parking lot. I haven't even absorbed this yet and notice other not-so-subtle changes that have taken place here since my last visit many months ago.

There's a tacky addition of three massive suction-cup affixed signs stuck directly on the window obstructing the view.

These are large, unruly signs that demand reading—like graffiti scrawled on your own porch.

And white letters, more paint and graffiti literally cover the bus shelter. Why would someone do that?

Then there's the little flowerbed smack-dab in front of the window here that used to win community beautification awards and was, at one time the pride of, well, somebody.

It's overgrown and full of garbage, debris and weeds.

These cold tracks of time don't seem like progress, just damage.

The removal of green grass for a parking lot; garish, huge hunks of advertising placed on the window, the bus stop glass completely covered in the artistic crimes of some wayward adolescent and the final insult, apathy and trash filling the once beautiful flowerbed, all point toward some kind of awful campaign of chaos.

It looks like ruin, selfish expression and just more inevitable explosions of change.

All of this makes me so sad, so angry that I get up to leave, but a tug at my heart causes me to stop and sit back down.

I sit, wait, look and think about all I see, and think and pray and think some more.

Change.

Change is unavoidable.

Change simply has to come.

If things don't change, things don't grow.

When things don't grow, they die.

When life sits still and becomes stagnant, it becomes difficult and unpleasant, like swimming in sewage.

Whether I like it or not, change just *is*.

I hear the still small, familiar voice of God inside, encouraging me to appreciate the past, learn from it, but not live there.

Sometimes I get a little tired of the fact that life is a series of changing moments that all add up to today but that's what we have, good or bad. We can control a few of those moments, but every one of them adds or subtracts from this moment, this right now, *this* today.

My first reactions, I'm learning, are usually not the best to lead with.

I could try to fight it.

I could complain and dwell on how tacky it looks, could get really mad, but doing that would only make it worse.

I need to put a new mental spin on all this, but don't really know how, so I guess I'll continue to sit here until something begins to click.

…and so I sit some more.

After a time it occurs to me that maybe that ugly new parking lot frees up parking on the street making things less crowded here; those signs on the window might help bring business in which would keep this little place going a little while longer and the more I look at it, the more the graffiti looks like someone's sad, overbearing way to tell the world to notice them. Plus, the once-beautiful flowerbed is still a flowerbed.

The bulbs under the surface just can't be seen yet, and besides, all that garbage isn't permanent because garbage is removable.

The flower garden also tells that anything not given care and attention will deteriorate when ignored, and that includes relationships, health, our integrity, our environment and everything else.

It's up to me whether I weed out and clean up old garbage-filled flowerbeds and decide to scrub off the graffiti placed in my past. I decide what to let grow there or get painted there today, and like my imaginary trip to my childhood earlier, I decide what to focus on from the past and whether that focus brings hope or bitterness.

So much is a matter of choice. We all decide what baggage we'll drag along and what is best to leave behind.

I'm choosing to let go of darkness and embrace the light. I'm choosing hope.

How my life or thoughts intersect...

Solitary Confinement

The mass of men lead lives of quiet desperation.

~ Henry David Thoreau

Winter

One college student with fresh crew cut and torn Army pants leans against the side of the bus shelter, but his head tilts down and his upper torso leans so far forward I'm afraid he might suddenly topple over onto the 30-something blonde who just sat down on the bench inside.

Upon sitting, 30-something immediately begins digging through a purse the size of a gunny sack. There he is, alone and there she is alone, both inside the bus shelter.

The woman intermittently stops searching, blankly stares in the opposite direction as if she's trying to picture just what on earth it was she was searching for in the first place and then peers into the purse again, continuing her efforts of excavation.

A rotund man approaches the bench, snorts, stops, coughs, spits on the sidewalk and to finish off his impressive entrance, explosively sneezes into the crook of his arm.

250

The blonde's back suddenly becomes rigid, her body language screaming, *Don't sit by me!* Maybe he gets the message, because Mr. Nasal Drainage stops short and turns, stopping just outside the shelter opposite from Army Pants Man on the other side.

Army Pants must have dozed off while standing, because at the sound of the rattling cough and spitting, for a nanosecond he pitches forward and almost falls face-first into the gaping, bottomless handbag before him. He snaps to a kind of weird attention, surveys himself and decides to correct his stance, probably to get more comfortable or look a bit cooler than he did as a leaning tower.

Thirty-Something finds a wayward tube of something and squirts some of the contents into the palms of her hands, rubbing them vigorously and applying the lotion or medicine to her neck and nose.

Mr. Nasal stares off in the opposite direction.

All turned inward.

All turned away.

All alone and serving time in self-induced solitary confinement.

I think we tend to relegate our attentions away in situations like this because opening internal doors could signal others to try to walk in and that has the potential to be weird, or uncomfortable; so we tend to deal with objects and usually not the other people brushing by.

A shopping bag from a high-end clothing store and latte arrive with a young woman and a backpack and beret atop the bright red hair of a man somewhere in his fifties, turn the corner and slow to a stop. All are close, but far enough away from everyone others to avoid entering their space, whatever that is.

Suddenly, the sky begins to toss a drop of rain here and there.

Latte Lady and Beret Man begin to make small steps toward the bus shelter, kinda-sorta sauntering as both look up and hold out a hand to the sky, showing the world the only reason they're going to get so close to any of the rest of them is, *Well, it's raining and I can't stand out here and get soaked.*

They stand just outside it when they arrive because it's pretty crowded.

Army Pants and Mr. Nasal bend and peer out of the bus shelter almost in unison, looking anxious for the bus to arrive, while a work boots and wool shirt stands in the rain like he doesn't care one little bit about getting soaked. Those inside scrunch up together so everyone can stay as dry as possible.

When the downpour really kicks in, Work Boots and a late arrival with an umbrella are just outside. Maybe they think coping with the chill of rain is better than standing buttock to buttock in the bus shelter with strangers in a forced setting of instant intimacy.

Umbrella Lady offers cover to Work Boots and he just shakes his head, *nah-h.*

At first, those inside the bus shelter look awkward and strange as nods and gestures indicate communication about the rain. The longer those in the shelter are forced into close proximity it's like the shower washes away walls of separation and pockets of ice, like springtime just arrived.

Now, it begins to really pour and even Work Boots tries to find cover which makes him laugh and shake his head, like man, *I don't know why I stood out there so dang long,* which causes nodding agreement about the doggone sogginess of it all that spreads in smiles and more scrunching together.

The drenching from the sky continues to melt walls.

As this happens, the bus stop and inhabitants cease to look so much like a frozen forest and take on a little warmth because these people now have this one thing, this blasted rain, this one struggle, this wonderful rain connection in common.

They're sharing something together, and have found their union, their tie and their bond and they aren't alone in their worlds anymore.

Then, I see the bus rounding the corner and watch as it pulls to the curb.

Connections shatter as the bus comes to a stop, and doors open.

Most of the sheltered folk stop all conversation and get ready to board the bus, but Sneezer and Army Pants are still chatting as they get on.

The cloudburst begins to subside a little while after the bus leaves and slowly, other passengers begin to collect at the bus stop.

A cowboy hat, thermos and rain gear arrive, followed by a longhaired man with an uncomfortable suit on and an earth woman with a baby in some baby-in-a-bag sling-thing.

They stand and sit far apart, just as the others had done, but this time, the rain clouds are gone.

There's no connection now.

Solitary confinement.

How my life or thoughts intersect...

<u>Rain</u>

Tiny rivers dot and paint windshields with clear,
          as the outside world
transforms to
          deeper greens,
          gravel glistens and
          dirty cars begin to shimmer
and shine.

Shoppers duck and cover,
          backpacks, envelopes and handbags used as poor
umbrellas

to keep from being touched
to keep from being
    affected
        by the rain.

But all of the effort cannot
prevent
its
falling.

The Rain Will Come.

Sooner or later,
it will head this way,
the dark,
pounding thunder
and torrents of raining sorrow

             will arrive again.

The questions then become,
    what do I do when the sun shines?
  and
    whom will I become
      as a result
      of
      the storm?

How my life or thoughts intersect...

Mom Shifts

When I approach a child, he inspires in me two sentiments; tenderness for what he is, and respect for what he may become.

~ Louis Pasteur

Early Spring

Two little boys play quietly with toys at a table seated with an ultra-busy, obviously active, sporty Mom-on-her-phone.

She is posh; she is a classy woman-on-the-go who, for the moment, doesn't appear to be able to see that babies are babies for just one quick breath.

While she talks banking and discusses *what's on your plate?* with the executive or business person on the other end of the line, her sons busy themselves and it is clear she is getting things done and making things happen in the world of commerce.

The boys play alone, saying softly, *Mamma, look at this! Mamma, he's a fighter pilot! Mamma! See what I can draw today?* as she ignores them, not once looking their way.

She doesn't stop talking. Her sons are invisible.

The two young boys continue their well-mannered play as the woman talks with an unknown caller, chuckles smarmily and then talks some more. With one call done, she speaks one sharp sentence of reprimand to her sons about the noise they create and calls someone else.

When parents are too busy, too important or too self-consumed with business, worry or their own bodily exercise to truly see the miracles toddling to adulthood before their eyes it feels to me like a tragedy.

The woman talks long and loud, sitting there in her expensive jogger's business suit, while ignoring the little ones who just want to connect with their mom and be part of her world.

She talks and talks and talks and talks, glaring and shaking her head at her boys before tapping a button on the cell phone and ending her conversation.

Now, all are silent.

The boys look at her with wide eyes and blink.

She looks down at her phone and back and forth, uncomfortable, as if trying to think of someone else to call.

Then suddenly, I can actually see it in her face and body language, a shifting begins.

At first, she appears lost, as if to say *What do I do with these little people?*

She is left with two simple young children who speak simple words and have simple questions and for a moment it seems she is still spinning in the magic land of Better Than This, and she doesn't seem up to the task of returning to a place where children live.

The gears grind for a while before this precious place and time can be truly seen and heard.

I actually watch the light enters her eyes. It begins to glow into a smile as she finally turns to see and truly hear her children again.

Mamma, look, I drew a train!

A strained moment passes. Finally, the mother speaks to her youngest boy, smiling, *Yes, that's a nice train! And look what a good helper brother is....*

In a world that would try to demean her role in these young men's lives and place the word *just* in front of the title she wears as mother; in a world that would tell her she simply isn't whole unless she's doing *anything* other than actively loving and raising her family, this woman—though swept away for a time—now smiles and plays with her sons and shows there's a mother's heart beating inside after all, and that's just enough light to give me a little hope for the whole wide   world.

How my life or thoughts intersect...

Unleashed

I think everybody should get rich and famous and do everything they ever dreamed of so they can see that it's not the answer.

~ Jim Carrey

Autumn

What made them decide to put a large screen television in the back of this nice little café and when did they do it?

Gaak.

It's been blaring loudly since I came in, and all I can think is *ugh...too bad.*

Finishing my lunch, the imposing thing recites and relives every detail of the latest Starlet Behaving Badly who is heading to rehab—again.

Like flame vs. moth, all eyes in here, including my own, focus on the train wreck of a story depicting the train wreck of a life, and as it does the warm hues of autumn leaves outside disappear, the people walking past or in and out of this café fade away as I, like a wide-eyed cod, stare at the screen like it's bait on a steel hook.

The flickering eye of a television set can wink me away from books I'm reading, songs I'm listening to, adventures I'd like to have, things I'd like to see…

I'm sure there are brain studies describing their magnetic draw, but whatever it is there are days when I want to throw televisions and computers out of my life because of the real living that doesn't take place when I'm connected to them.

Yes, they can be the conduit of discoveries and entertainment, but there are days when it feels like that's a bad trade for really living.

And how strange is it that these machines cause us to feel connected to perfect strangers like this sad movie star?

We've heard these strangers' names, seen their movies, listened to their music and because of that, we feel like we've spent time with them when we haven't.

Maybe we pay so much attention to their broken places because we don't feel so comfortable staring into our own.

Looking around the café as the sad story continues to unfold, it's clear that none of us in here are famous and nothing we do to self-destruct will hit the evening news unless it results in something criminal, but I sure hope every one of us is a celebrity to someone.

I move my chair back to face the window just in time to see an extremely tall woman with short, pinkish-blonde hair that sticks straight up go shooting past the window. With her jaw set in an expression of raw determination and her upper torso rigid, she seems to water-ski by as four little rat-terriers pull, *yap*, pull, *yap*, pull, *yap* and yank her arms in strange directions as she somehow maneuvers this force of nature across the street and down the block.

What a peculiar, wondrous and sensational sight.

Maybe this is her job as a dog-walker or if she owns the manic little herd, a tortuous form of mutual exercise; yet what cuts in front of traffic and zooms up the hill seems less and less like that and more and more like some kind of *event.*

Watching the furious barking tangle of canine and human vs. leashes and fur careening along, it honestly feels more like members of a parade got lost and wandered off course and are frantically looking for the Clydesdales or marching band they were behind so they can hop back in parade line.

The whole thing is delightful and just a little frightening.

Like so many things that happen outside this window, as I sit here trying to recreate the image in my mind it's hard to believe it was real. It's also hard to believe there's any sensible way to combine what first greeted me here today and the goofy scene that exploded past the window just now, but somehow there is.

Ah yes, and here it comes…

There will always be incessant, yapping distractions that can drag each of us by the wrists, mind and soul—famous or not—to do things we *think* we want to do, but in the end just bring loss and destruction.

Maybe the addict-actress-now-in-rehab would agree today.

The little barking things we sometimes invite in usually don't seem too bad one at a time, but when allowed to pile up and gang up, they can pull us off our path and rob us of our dreams.

The news is full of stories of those who have never found it again.

Whether the little thing seems good or bad, if it's dragging us out of kilter with the rest of our lives it's time to step back, pray and take a good long look at it. It might be best to unleash it or turn it off before it yanks us away from our parade and drags us somewhere we were never meant to be.

The first step, the very first step to being free of it all is to identify who or what is pulling on the lead.

How my life or thoughts intersect...

The Books We Are

Happiness is not a station you arrive at,
but a manner of traveling.

- Margaret Lee Runbeck

Early Spring

The view outside has changed over time and most of the people going past aren't the same who walked by almost twenty years ago when I first came in, but how it feels to be here is still the same.

It always feels like coming home and it still seems like I've met them all somewhere before.

Like right now, over by the bus stop, a 40-something man rests in green grass with an obviously engrossing book.

A long-haired younger backpack-toting man carries a plastic milk crate past a tired mom in a jacket not quite covering a waitress uniform, she shakes her head at someone's active wild child who busies himself by ricocheting off tree trunks and anything else in his path. A heavy-set middle-aged man in sweats carries a new-looking gym bag onto the bus as another middle aged man wearing dirty work clothes sits in the bus shelter with his lunch box at his side and a day's labor on his shoulders and face.

Just across the street stands a grandpa-man who probably wouldn't want to know his awkward fumbling with an iPod is kind of cute.

An earth-loving vegan who wears a t-shirt broadcasting this rolls an old, beat-up bicycle past two teenagers pushing a stroller.

A retired-age dad and his younger image son walk past my window laughing between frosty bites of ice-cream cones and I find no words to describe the beauty of the two.

We are, each of us a marvelous chapter in the book of the world.

We all provide vital parts of the plot and story line.

None of us will ever know the depth and scope of the lessons each life has on those who witness it, but each one of us hides treasure, storehouses and stories waiting to be discovered like lovely old books.

And look at us. We're all just people. We're all just us.

Each in our own way, we're trying to live our own lives the best we can with who we are and the nature and nurturing we were handed.

Just people.

All of us.

No matter what our abilities, work history, age, level of education, religious affiliation, habits, IQ, addictions, nationality, hobbies, sexual orientation, nervous tics, levels of love or abuse, physical state, attitude, political affiliation, experience, skin color, hair color, nail color or what thickness of toilet paper we like best, we are all just wandering, wondering—and when we dig past the damage—strange and intricate people.

The air we breathe, the history of our planet and the fact that we deal with all this human stuff together connects us. All of us. We all live under the same sun and moon whether we can see them or not, and most of us know what it's like to feel frightened and alone.

We share so much.

Connections.

We may speak different languages, or be from different eras. Some have had to deal with torturous misery while some have had life pretty easy. Damage and misunderstanding create behaviors most of us don't understand, but we can still offer each other respect.

We come from different cultures and sub-cultures, mansions, suburbs, tents or trailer parks, yet what connects us is bigger and I've learned here on this corner that those connections are more important than anything that could ever divide us.

Besides, how can *Who We Are Now* matter when, whether we take an active part in the process or not, we're always becoming something different, something far more?

We decide if we become more of what we've always been, what we settle for or more of who we were always destined to be by taking the hard look inside without blaming anyone else for who we are.

This life is no competition, no race.

We just are—and the reality is, as long as we're all drawing breath, we honest-to-God, are in this deal together.

How my life or thoughts intersect...

The Last Secret

All the art of living lies in a fine mingling
of letting go and holding on.

~ Henry Ellis

Late Spring

I take a different route to my favorite lookout and café today.

A truck runs the stop sign and I lay on the horn, distracted as I pull into a parking place in front of the café. Scattered and shaken, opening the car door, I shield my eyes against a rogue gust of wind and dust.

An ominous feeling follows me inside my special corner of the world.

Walking directly to the counter on the far side of the room I place my order and turn back toward the window, and when I finally look up I freeze as I try to take in what I see on the opposite side of the street. Distraction or no, how did I not see this driving in? Blinking hard, I try to shake the sight from my eyes.

The peaceful space I have been drawn to and have loved for so many years is now a ravaged stranger.

Black plastic and crude wooden stakes replace all of the soft green grass and create a fence encircling the area beside the fire station. This is the place where innocence danced and the summer sun-catchers rested and read before buses arrived.

Now, some prehistoric creature-like earth-moving machine has stripped her of any green except for the lone pine tree. Old Christmas lights are still hidden in her branches and she stands in the center of the dirt and rock like a lost child.

The bus stop is gone.

Temporary stops have been designated across the street and it looks like there's another one across from the school.

In the direction of the old furniture store at least six large, beautiful old trees including a huge cherry tree and all the other giants that lined the street across from my viewpoint here have been recently cut down, with only man-tall stubs of life left. They must have needed a bigger saw to cut through the large trunks that now stand as severed sentinels.

No promise of delicate pink blossoms announcing springtime or swirling like snow in the cool wind here again, no more shade from their rich green leaves in summer heat--just freshly cut stumps left to weep in the springtime sun.

Right now, workmen in garish orange and yellow vests survey and spray ugly neon-colored paint here and there, as emotions crash inside my skull until all I can think is, *please stop, please, just stop...* and I remember the smiling cartoon image of the moving man once displayed and can't help but wish he was there now, that he would come tell me this is all a bad joke and make everything like it used to be.

I want to scream against this destruction, beg them to just stop and leave it all alone, but it it's already too late.

Proof of more to come, road signs and orange cones, are piled in the staff parking lot beside the courthouse all ready to offer instructions on how we'll need to navigate the next phase of the "improvements."

Like an aberrant sideshow, the neon-toting workmen continue to parade back and forth, but I can't watch them measure, carve or dismember my hometown friend any longer and can't hold back my tears.

As with the rest of life, we all know change is coming but dear God, we are never truly prepared for the moment it arrives.

Though I want to run, I decide to collect myself a moment and sit down to eat a couple bites of soup.

Though I am determined to ignore the destruction in front of me, some movement by the new makeshift bus stop catches my eye.

A young father with a super-deluxe, four-wheel drive stroller rolls past Orange Vest Surveyor and Measuring Tape Man without even glancing at what they are doing.

He maneuvers himself and his child along the sidewalk and as he passes a suit-clad older man with briefcase, both look up and exchange friendly nods.

They're standing in the middle of complete destruction and they don't even see it. I don't know what I expect them to do, but it is as if they are completely oblivious to their surroundings and only see the humanity in each other walking by. It's a small spark, but a hopeful spark just the same.

A bus pulls up at the corner and an unkempt, angry-looking man in his mid-twenties steps off with dirty black hair poking out from under the black hood of his sweatshirt.

His glasses, beard, shorts, socks, shoes and backpack—all night-sky black, and I think, *Depressing, dirty guy, great.*

Mindlessly watching him as he crosses the street and walks my direction, I dislike his intrusion on the one tiny ray of hope here but for some reason I don't look away.

I wish he would walk the other direction, take all this dark wreckage with him and *just get the hell out here*, but I can't stop watching him.

As he continues walking toward me, his thumbs unhook from his backpack straps revealing four five-inch tall white block letters on his t-shirt spelling out a word that stands out like neon in the blackest night.

He holds his hands open, like he's some kind of messenger sent here to show me this particular word on this particular day in this particular place.

Today of all days, to see this, especially in light of recent tragic loss in my family, well, it pops the gloom like an overfilled balloon.

The word he wears represents to me the uncomplicated constant that transcends all of this, the one thing that remains secure, never turns away, never grows old or ceases to be, never gets demolished or cut down, never leaves, never misunderstands, never forgets and never dies.

The word he displays is the only thing on this earth that is dependable and completely immune to the relentless tides of change.

The big, bright writing on the young man's chest is simply the word ***love.***

No, I'm not Pollyanna and no, I'm not kidding.

In this moment, it doesn't just symbolize the limited, unreliable and often goofy kind of love we humans are able to offer, but the bedrock of that, the foundation of existence itself; the timeless love that generated everything to begin with.

Simple? Yes.

Simplistic? No.

Being reminded of it today, as the word interlaces itself through so many emotions and memories here, this day now feels like the finale' of a beautiful song.

As the young man and his message continue down the sidewalk I realize the melody is the reality that there is no dream, ideal, job, pain, person, situation, success, or tragic circumstance more powerful than that limitless love and grace that brought us all here in the first place.

Without it life is a war-torn landscape, a difficult, impossibly harsh experience spent in pursuit of vapor and things that don't last; but when that forever God-love is allowed in, pain transforms to purpose, broken places lose sharp edges, lost dreams are reborn and healing begins.

A bus pulls up two blocks past the devastation and a small group board. They're far away and their faces become every face from every visit I have ever made here; the elderly woman who walked to the store, the grandpa, the blind man, the friends, joggers, drivers, bikers, walkers, mothers, sisters, brothers, fathers, sons, daughters, all of them...

Smokescreens dissipate and a secret emerges as if from the dust and residue outside:

One way or another, we're all just trying to do the best we can with who we are. We're all just vulnerable, damaged, fallible people stumbling around in the dark with incomplete blueprints, struggling to find the light switch.

But the secret is the light was never off—it's been there, bright and shining all along.

This world is different than it was over twenty years ago when I first began coming to Jackson and Main, but then it's also still very much the same.

In spite of all the changes, and so often, because of them, we will still go just as far as we allow love and relationship to take us.

That's it.

That's all.

That's enough.

That's abundance.

That's the stuff of life.

After I pack my things and ready to drive away I decide to circle the block just once to say good-bye.

Past the intersection—honest-to-God—there by the temporary bus stop stands an older grandpa-man, peeking in and looking for pop cans in the new garbage can.

Just as unbelievably, as I finally turn to drive away from my corner, past the surveyors and yellow tape to head home, an unshaven older man stands crookedly just up the street in dirty, torn pants and a work-worn jacket.

He stops in his tracks and looks directly at me.

I bring my car to a crawl and can see that under the shade of his tattered brown hat a jagged, broad smile appears. He slowly raises one arm and waves as he nods at me.

I slow to a momentary stop and feel as if I will laugh and cry all at the same time, trying to take this all in, I manage a smile and wave, the image of him unfading, I see him in the rearview mirror as I continue on my way.

~

Whatever it is that began here more than twenty years ago, whatever I was destined to discover here is finished today.

I have the strange and wonderful sense that the entire world has become Jackson & Main and though it's sad to think my visits to this special corner of the world may be over, I believe something absolutely incredible has just begun.

Every story, every puzzle piece has fallen into place, because as I drive, leaving the intersection of Jackson and Main streets far behind I finally understand what I was drawn here to find.

The secret of life itself has nothing to do with how we look, what we own, what we do for a living or where we go.

When all is said and done, when we've drawn our final breath and are looking back on days spent like currency, it's the love offered up in the little moments of every day that give meaning to life.

Living is relationship and relationships take time, respect, thought and effort. It's in relationship that we grow and become the *me* we've been destined to become from the beginning.

That's where life happens, in all the little things like love and grace that are given, taken and shared.

Looks like it's true. Little things have never been little at all.

About the Author

Lindy Barr Batdorf still drives by Jackson & Main from time to time and keeps busy writing, voice acting, observing, researching, spending time with friends and family and loving life.

The restaurant where this book was written is closed as of this writing and the building on her magical corner has butcher paper on the windows awaiting some exciting surprise.

Lindy and her husband Alan of almost 40 years, have two grown sons, rescue animals and are on a never-ending adventure to find the miracles hidden within the everyday.

Also by Lindy Barr Batdorf:

Stop and Smell the Asphalt:
Laughter and love along the highway of Parenthood.

Coming soon:
The Dreamer's Book of Secrets
A handbook for creative souls
and
Heartsounds:
A journey of Hope and Healing
~

Contact information:

Batdorf Communications
P.O. Box 3054
Clackamas, OR 97015

Facebook:
Jackson & Main: *Meditations and Everyday Miracles*

All photographs in this book were taken and edited by the author,
Lindy Barr Batdorf, on or near Jackson & Main.